SOMETHING TO SAY
TO THE CONGREGATION

SOMETHING TO SAY TO THE CONGREGATION

———————— · ————————

John R. Gray

Edited by Sheila Gray

———————— · ————————

T&T CLARK
EDINBURGH

T&T CLARK
59 GEORGE STREET
EDINBURGH EH2 2LQ
SCOTLAND

First Published 1991

ISBN 0 567 29200 2

British Library Cataloguing in Publication Data

A Catalogue record for this book is
available from the British Library

Typeset by Trinity Typesetting, Edinburgh.
Printed and bound in Great Britain by Billing & Son Ltd, Worcester.

INTRODUCTION

"Who, having been called to be a preacher, would stoop to be a king?" So said Thomas Carlyle and so frequently echoed the man who preached these sermons.

John Gray played many parts in his life — scholar, war-time naval chaplain, rather unwilling member of Assembly committees, Moderator of the General Assembly of the Church of Scotland, but above all else he was a parish minister — a pastor and preacher. He loved his calling and he loved people, especially his two congregations in the city centre of Glasgow and Dunblane Cathedral.

He had a great affection for and understanding of his fellow workers in the parish ministry, knowing from experience the strains they are under. He knew the feeling of despair at the end of a week which had been so full of the necessary, but time-consuming, minutiae of parish work that there had been no time for sermon preparation — or even when a streaming cold had driven away all desire to preach the Gospel ever again! Those were the times when he would turn to the books of sermons of an earlier generation, not to be reproduced verbatim, of course, but just in the search for an idea to be worked on in his own way and in his own words.

I hope this book may help, in the same way, to give some ideas and inspiration to John's successors in today's pulpits. For they too have to have "something to say to the congregation".

The contents are drawn from the sermons which I found after John's death in 1984. Most of them were preached in Glasgow or Dunblane during the last twenty years of his life. I have chosen as wide a variety as possible. I can only hope that I have chosen as he would have wished, although he and I sometimes disagreed as to the quality of a sermon. He was his own harshest critic. I can almost hear him say, "Why did you include that one, Sheila — it wasn't worth printing."

The sermons are more or less as John preached them, which means that they contain some of the repetitions and colloquialisms which gave his spoken message its drawing power. I have taken out some purely local illustrations, and have updated others — it would not be helpful, for example, to find references to the "unending Vietnam War", but the changes are minimal. Other sermons had been "tidied up" by John himself, for publication in the *Expository Times*.

One or two sermons, which I found in a separate package, had been prepared by him as the basis of a proposed book. It was one of the sorrows of his life that he was never able to take the time to complete it. I have tried to do that for him, as a labour of love.

Preaching must be, like everything else in life, an on-going process, ever open to new forms and new ideas and new interpretations. The preachers of today and tomorrow cannot be shackled to the concepts and methods of a past generation. That would be the last thing that John would have wished — his own style and length of sermon changed with the times and with the needs of his listeners. He would have been very interested to have seen how the new generation copes with the problems of exegesis. But the God who through the centuries has inspired the born preacher and the less gifted alike, does not change. His Word, as seen in Jesus Christ, is for all and for all time.

I pray that the ideas of a man who served his Saviour faithfully in his own day, may ease the task of those who bear the heat and burden of *this* day and of days to come.

CONTENTS

SERMONS FOR THE CHURCH'S YEAR

ADVENT

God's Kingdom the First Choice

Matthew 6.33 (NEB) "Set your mind on God's kingdom —
before everything else."

There is a story told of a French soldier who was shot during
the Napoleonic wars. The bullet was lodged somewhere near
his heart. As the surgeon probed for it, the soldier quipped "Be
careful or you'll cut the Emperor", suggesting that Napoleon
was to be found at the very centre of his being. Accepting this
metaphor, what would the surgeon find if his scalpel slipped
and he cut open *our* hearts? Perhaps he would come across a
bank balance, a squash racquet, a political manifesto, a house, a
garden or another human being. What is your dominant interest,
the ruling passion of your lives? Is it business, house, sport,
money, husband, wife, child? Around what or whom is your
life organised, to which all else is subordinate? Often people
use a revealing phrase — "He just lived for his work" or "She
just lived for her children." Nothing else mattered.

There is a parlour game which the psychologists have
invented called "The Chain Reaction Test". You set a number
of people down with paper and pencil, and start them off
with a word. Then tell them to write down whatever words
come into their heads. The results are often revealing. Start
where you will, say with the word "church", people reveal the
dominant concern of their lives. The mother, perhaps, moves
from "church" to "marriage" to "baptism" to "babies". The
financier from church will move to "collection" to "balance
sheet", the architect from "church" to "building" to "hall" to
"house" and so on. Each will reveal the dominant interest of
their lives. What is yours? Round what do you organise your
life? What gives meaning to it?

3

If it is any of the things of which I have spoken — money, business, sport, house or child, then you are at constant risk of suddenly finding life drained of meaning. Any business can collapse; any child can disappoint; a loved one may die; sport becomes impossible with age; a house, once a delight, can become a burden.

This is the first Sunday in Advent. Advent reminds us that every human effort or achievement will be brought before the judgement of God. Indeed, sooner or later the foolishness, or at least the inadequacy, of every worldly purpose becomes apparent to ourselves. Andrew Carnegie, Isaac Wolfson, Lord Nuffield, all having spent a lifetime making money, suddenly felt how foolish it had all been and began to give it away, much as a child demolishes the sandcastle before the tide sweeps it away. The ideal would be to find a purpose which would be independant of the chances and swift changes of this uncertain life and would last through youth and age, through health and sickness, through good days and bad, through joy and sorrow.

Our fathers were quite clear that they had such a purpose. "Man's chief end is to glorify God and enjoy Him for ever."

"Set your mind on God's kingdom" said Jesus, "before everything else." Of course it is not easy. Work, money, health, home and family are important. None knew that better than Christ, who asked us to pray for daily bread, and taught us to find in our human loves the reflection of the love of God and to serve Him chiefly in the service of others.

Of course we all have our hierarchy of values — sport meaning more to one, music to another, gardening to someone else. There is no reason why we should all be alike in what we put second, third, fourth and fifth in our lives. But, if there be a God, what else can be first, save His will and purpose? Surely to accept any purpose less good than the best, any aim lower than the highest is madness. It is as simple as that. But not of course easy.

That is why all we are asked to do is to set our *minds* on — not *find* — the Kingdom of God. It is not a present possession, but only a purpose, a search rather than an achievement. But it is a search from which there is no respite. It is not a case of giving your vote for God and leaving it at that. It means hour by hour and day by day seeking God's will and doing it, rejecting every alternative. It means very often choosing that which is in conflict with every desire, every instinct, against which your heart and soul rebel, for which there is no argument save the fact that it *is* God's will. It is not easy.

Jesus did not find it so. He shows that in Gethsemane where He made the final choice. Only by a supreme effort was He finally able to cry "Not as I will, but as Thou wilt."

May we be delivered from a dilemma so dreadful and agonising. But only if we are prepared to face such a choice and make the same decision as Christ made, will we choose aright in the thousand dilemmas which confront us day by day. Where shall be find strength to choose God's way rather than our way? Only where Christ found it, in seeing that the rule of God is the will of our Father; in seeing behind the blank fearsomeness of life and death, a wise and gentle love.

"My times are in thy hand;
Why should I doubt or fear?
My Father's hand will never cause
His child a needless tear."

Christ did not yield to the judgement of an inscrutable providence. He accepted the will of the Heavenly Father. It was because He began "Father" that He went on to say "Not my will, but thine be done." Set your mind on God's kingdom — *before everything else*" means nothing other than the rule of the Father's Love.

Christ the Hope of Glory

Colossians 1.27 "Christ — in you — the hope of glory."

What is this season of Advent that comes just before Christmas? What does it do? What is it meant to do?

It points back to something that happened, which really and truly happened. The unrepeatable mighty act of God who sent His Son, an act the greater of which cannot be imagined. Nearly 2000 years ago, the event which had been hoped for, longed for, prayed for, waited for — that event happened. Since the first baby cry was heard in the Bethlehem stable, the world has never been the same and never will be. In some ways, the whole world knows this and acknowledges it. Not only does the year hinge on this event, but so does all history. BC-AD! Christ has come. That is not to be doubted or denied or reversed or repeated, and that coming of Christ has made a difference. Wherever He has become known, the true and good and the beautiful have flourished, and cruel and wicked things have vanished like evil beasts at the rising of the sun. Slavery is at an end where Christ is known — and human sacrifice and canibalism and the unspeakable things that have ravished souls for a million years.

So much has been accomplished. Don't let us forget that or make light of it. So much has been done but so much more remains to be done. Not only is Christ unknown in over half the world but in the half in which He is acknowledged, the extent of man's allegiance is minute. Think of the incredible brutalities in Northern Ireland and the Middle East or of famine and wretchedness in Africa and South America. And think of how little we do about it except to congratulate ourselves that we are well out of it all. The power of God has been made free to us for twenty centuries and how pitifully little it has affected us. In an average town we give far less per year to Christian Aid than we spend on food for our dogs and cats. In Britain we give 3 per cent of our gross national product in Aid, far less than we spend on drink and on gambling. How is that for a Christian people? We keep 97 *per cent* of our wealth for ourselves!

One can hear Christ say in a bewildered way, "So you are Christians, called by my name. You have motor cars and television sets and food to eat and to waste, and your brothers and sisters are hungry. How can this be? You have had the knowledge of the Gospel for 2000 years."

Certain and final as Christ's coming was, He might as well not have come for all the difference He has made in many lands. Historic fact it may be, but it is still largely future expectation. The song of the angels is real enough but distant — a far off triumphant song. Glory, glory, hallelujah, but the glory is not so much something that has come as something that is promised — a promise of the day when the earth shall be full of the knowledge of God as the waters cover the sea; when the kingdoms of this world shall have become the kingdoms of our Lord and of His Christ.

And we, you and I, live between the times; between Christ's coming and Christ's victory. That victory will come, but whether it comes sooner or later depends on us. The end of the obscenities in Belfast and Londonderry, of all the injustices and cruelties and inhumanities will come — glory, glory hallelujah, the end will come, but will come not by the will of man nor the power of man nor by the wisdom of man. They are beyond that. They will end by the power of God released into His world by His people.

The hope of peace, of plenty, of justice and sanity, the hope of glory is the measure and degree in which that Christ made flesh long ago is made flesh again in your lives and mine. The only hope of sanity and order in the world is if there can be such an end of greed and suspicion as will come when Christ comes anew into the hearts of ordinary men and women. Christ in you.

The thing of course is impossible, that the Eternal Son of God, the King of Glory should be in you. Yet once it happened.

The Word was made flesh, the Saviour lay a baby in His Mother's arms and dwelt among us. The Hope of Glory is that in marvellous condescension and wondrous humility, He will come anew and dwell in you and me.

The Hope of Glory is Christ in you and me.

―――――― · ――――――

Christ Will Come Again

Matthew 24.36 "Of the day or hour knoweth no man, no, not the angels of heaven, but my Father only."

This is the season of Advent, when we remember two things — that our Lord came at the first Christmas, and that He promised to come again.

We are never more happy, never more at ease in the Church than at Christmas time. We accept with joy the story of how Christ first came into our world. We are never again unhappy, never again ill at ease with the promise that Christ will come again.

As C. S. Lewis pointed out, orthodox Christians have shied clear of this idea of the second coming of Christ because unorthodox Christians have made far too much of it. In the year AD 1000, the whole Christian world was in a turmoil expecting the world to end. Since then, little groups of earnest souls have, by means of elaborate calculations, convinced themselves and others that Christ would come at a certain hour on a certain date that has been revealed to them. Last century one William Miller persuaded large numbers of people that the Lord would appear at midnight on 21st March 1843. The Jehovah's Witnesses, basing their calculations on similarly isolated texts, make similar sorts of predictions.

Times like our own encourage this kind of wild speculation. It is all very sad and very silly. Yet the mistakes of fanatics should not blind us to the fact that Christ had some very clear and definite things to say on the point. C. S. Lewis sums up Christ's teaching in three clear propositions:

1. That Christ will certainly return.
2. That we cannot possibly find out when.
3. And that therefore we must always be ready for Him.

1. Christ will certainly return. A day will dawn that will not last to sunset. There have been cataclysms, accidents, mishaps in the universe before. There will be again. If such a thing happened, I might never finish this sentence. John Donne once asked "What if this were the world's last night?" Well, it may be, or of course, equally it may not. The world's last night may be billions of years away. But sooner or later the world will end and it will end not at a moment chosen by us but at a moment chosen by God. When it ends our whole lives, even the darkest and most obscure corners will be brought under the scrutiny of God. The criterion by which they will be judged is by the degree to which they correspond to the life and will and purpose of Christ.

The first coming of Christ was not brought about by a democratic vote. It was not arranged by a committee nor conceded as a result of a campaign. It did not happen by man's contriving. It happened when God chose. In the fulness of time, God sent His Son and the Word was made flesh. At the end of time, when God sees that it is right, He will send His Son to complete the work. The world with which we are familiar, with its buying and selling, its being born and dying, its politics and planning, its laughter and sorrow, seems very permanent. Sooner or later it will end. The great experiment of God will be complete.

What if this were the world's last night?

2. But, of course it probably won't be and we certainly have no means of knowing that it will. Christ most definitely and decisively said, not once or twice only "Of this day and hour no man knoweth. No, not the angels of heaven but my Father only."

Is it not obvious that it must be so? If once it were given to men to know the day and hour, the power of God would be limited, His freedom to deal as He sees best with the needs and sins and sorrows of men would be taken away. Moreover, which one of us could bear to know so much? We could not bear to know the hour and day and date of our own death or the death or those whom we love. To know the precise date of the end of the world would drive us insane. It would make the world, not a vale of soul-making but a place of soul-destruction.

Where the Jehovah's Witnesses and others who give a date to the Second Coming go wrong, is not in their calculations — foolish though these are — they go wrong in not trusting God. If we really believe in God and have come to Know Him in Christ as a God of Love, we shall be quite content to leave these final issues in His hands, where they belong.

You and I are actors on the stage of life — very minor characters at that. If we have confidence in the producer, we shall not want to tell Him His business. We should each of us be content to play our part as He directs, making our entrances and our exits as He decides, certain that He will bring the whole production to a happy and successful ending. The analogy, like all analogies, is not perfect but may suffice to illustrate how needful it is for us to leave the time of the final judgement in the hands of God. We do not and cannot and must not and are not meant to know what God has kept in His own hand.

Christ will come again.

We cannot know when — and therefore

3. We must always be ready for Him. That does not mean standing around idly in white garments, singing hymns. It means behaving in such a fashion that we shall not mind at what moment the end comes. For, of course, however many billions of years the world may have to run, none of us have much above three score years and ten, and all of us have a

week less than we had last Sunday. I sometimes smile when I accept engagements for a year or more ahead. It will not matter what plans we have made, what engagements we have entered into. Intolerable though it may seem, our little lives may be wound up at any time, without a moment's notice. We none of us have a lease of life — even for a day.

What if this were the world's last night, if you and I knew we would die before morning? How would we behave? How would it affect our attitude to our possessions? Would it change the amount of time and attention we give to our prayers? Would it alter the way we treat other people? Well, that is how you and I ought to treat our possessions, our prayers and other people, for so far as any of us is concerned, the world *may* end this very night.

If you want to sleep badly tonight, try and shut out the thought of death. If you want to sleep well, accept the fact that one day you must die.

Make your will.

Make your peace with your neighbours.

Make your peace with God,

and then commit yourself and those whom you love into His care and keeping, and fall asleep.

The recognition that for us, if not for everyone, this may be the world's last night should not lead us to gloom or fear, far less to hysteria or panic. It should lead us rather to quiet confidence and humble trust, sure that now, at the end, and thereafter for ever, we are not at the mercy of blind fate, nor controlled by cruel destiny, but are in the care of a Father's love. And so we can be content that "Of the day and hour knoweth no man, not the angels of heaven, but my Father only", sure that "My Father's hand will never cause his child a needless tear" and *glad* that "Of the day knoweth my Father."

Neither Ichabod, nor Ebenezer but Emmanuel

1 Samuel 4.21 "They named the child Ichabod, saying, 'The glory is departed from Israel'."
1 Samuel 7.12 "Samuel took a stone — naming it Ebenezer, 'for to this point the Lord has helped us'."
Matthew 1.23 "They shall call His name Emmanuel — God is with us."

When a new baby comes, there is nothing which causes more heart-searching, and sometimes more heart-burning, than the choice of a name.

Poor little Ichabod didn't come out of it very well. He got his name because he had the misfortune to be born at the lowest point in the fortunes of Israel — just after the Ark of the Covenant had been removed by the Philistines. It is difficult for us to realise what the Ark meant to the Jews. Externally it was nothing — a chest about 3 feet 9 inches long, covered with a golden lid called the Mercy seat on which were the figures of two Cherubims facing each other. Between the Cherubims was an empty place, its very emptiness the symbol of the Unseen God of Whom no image could be made. In the Ark were the tablets of stone with the Commandments engraved on them, Aaron's rod and a pot of manna.

Simple enough in itself, the Ark symbolised God's gracious dealings with Israel, His providing for their needs and His unchanging law. It had become not only the focus of national unity, but also a visible reminder of God's favour to His people. So when it was taken away men felt that Israel's great days were over. When Eli's grandson was born, his father dead and his mother dying in giving him birth, it seemed that the withdrawal of God's favour from Israel was complete, and so the little boy was called Ichabod, "the glory is departed from Israel."

But they need not have been so morose. The Ark did not remain long with the Philistines. It caused them so much trouble that they were glad to be rid of it. By the time Ichabod was grown up, the Ark was back in its place, the Philistines had been defeated and the wise Samuel was in charge of Israel's affairs. Looking back on all Israel's troubles, on the removal of the Ark and its restoration, on the attacks of the Philistines and on their final defeat, Samuel set up a stone and called it Ebenezer, "for to this point", he said, "the Lord has helped us."

In today's world, in our country and in the Church, there is no shortage of people ready to cry "Ichabod", "Glory has departed from Israel." When one looks back to the thirties, to the British Empire on which the sun never set, when drugs did not mean cannabis or heroine but Syrup of Figs or Gregory's Mixture, when the Church was sure of her faith and everywhere on the offensive, one might give a nostalgic sigh. Our fathers were so sure of their God and of their country's destiny. Now all is changed. In the Church membership is shrinking, partly because of weak leadership. In the world Britain seems to count for less and less all the time. The glory has departed from Israel, the Philistines are in the ascendant, the Ark of the Covenant has been spirited away. So we cry, many of us, — "Ichabod".

Yet, look a little deeper. All has not been loss in the past fifty years. Hitler's Naziism did not succeed — it is now only an ugly memory. We are healthier and longer-lived than our fathers were. The desperate poverty of the early thirties is gone. Slums are disappearing. We may not be at the peak of our power, but we've weathered the Depression and two World Wars. We were a lot nearer down and out at Dunkirk and somehow we won through. It may not be true that we've never had it so good, but we've had it a lot worse and survived.

And if the Church shows no great signs of advance, yet she has stood up better than any other institution to the acid attacks of modernity, and if there is less religion, what there is, is honest and genuine! There is a new hidden church of worshippers by radio and television. If there are snakes there are also ladders. If there are black squares on the board, there are as many white; and if some of the glory has departed from Israel, the glory was not all real, or at least it hid much that was also tawdry and false. So as we look back with the eye of faith, we are led not so much to cry "Ichabod" as to say "Ebenezer" — "To this point the Lord has helped us."

Yet, even Ebenezer is not the last word. There's a certain cautious scepticism about it, as if to say, "I'm bound to admit that the Lord has helped up to now, but, as for tomorrow, that is another question." Ichabod and Ebenezer both reflect that backward look in which there is more than a trace of atheism. But *God is not dead*. His best days are not over. Neither Ichabod nor Ebenezer is adequate. God is not the God of our fathers only, but of our children. He is the God of their tomorrows as He was of our yesterdays. For He has promised, and He is faithful that promised to be our God and the God of our children unto all generations.

Two thousand years ago a new born baby's cry was heard in Bethlehem and His name was Emmanuel — God with us. From that child, when He was grown, people learned that God was no tyrant, ready to desert his people at the first hint of disobedience, nor even One who from a distance was willing to help the penitent. In Christ they found One who was ready and eager to share their sorrows, their loneliness, their temptations and even their death; who was willing to accompany them in all the perplexing paths of life, even through the deep dark valley, and who would be ready to welcome them on the other side. We cannot tell what the future into which our children will grow will be like — as unlike the present, probably, as the present is unlike the past. This we can be sure of, that it will be as full of God as ever was the past. We who have discovered the nature and the Love of God in Jesus Christ, know that of that Love there is no end. "Lo", Christ said, "I am with you always, even to the end."

As the Psalmist said:
> "Yea, tho' I walk through death's dark vale
> Yet will I fear no ill,
> For Thou art with me
> And Thy rod and staff me comfort still."

The anguish of "Ichabod", the caution of "Ebenezer", are swallowed up in the calm and triumphant assurance of "Emmanuel — God with us".

CHRISTMAS EVE

Travellers

Christmas is a great time for travelling — for going home or for going from home. Some of you made a long journey to be here, and many of you will tomorrow be going to visit friends and relatives or will be welcoming those who have come to see you. There is something appropriate in this and something appropriate too, in the concern most of us feel for strangers and travellers at Christmas time.

For, if you think of it, none of those involved in the first Christmas were at home. Mary and Joseph, the victims of a harsh bureaucracy, had to make a journey from Nazareth to Bethlehem, about 70 or 80 miles through the mountains. It must have been an anxious, wearing journey and with no welcome at the journey's end.

The shepherds too seem to have had quite a long journey down from the mountain to the city. "Let us go now" they said, "even unto Bethlehem" — "All the way to Bethlehem" as we might say — "to see this thing which has come to pass."

The Wise Men journeyed from Persia, or perhaps from India or even China. It had perhaps taken them weeks or months, and scholarly people are not fond of the rigours of travel.

It *is* odd, when one thinks of it. Mary and Joseph from the North, the wise men from the East and the shepherds from the hills, all converging on the tiny inn, their journey ending at the makeshift cradle. And One had made the furthest journey of all — Christ the Son of God, Who had come from highest heaven to live among men on earth.

We human beings, especially we British, are conceited folk. We are apt to think of ourselves as the centre of all things. We measure east and west by a line which runs through

16

Greenwich; the time by which we judge all other times is Greenwich Mean Time. When there is fog in the Channel, the headlines are not that Britain is cut off from the Continent, but that the Continent is cut off from Britain.

In the same way, we think of the world as the centre of the universe and of God as living in some remote suburb, so that when He came to earth it must have been rather fun for Him! The truth is the opposite — God is the centre and when He came in Christ, He came in love to an insignificant planet — earth — to the insignificant town of Bethlehem and to an insignificant peasant girl. Could condescension go further, and could there be justification for such condescension, save for some mighty purpose — for the salvation of the world? When God came in Christ, He came the longest journey of all, as far as the east is from the west, as far as Heaven is high above the Earth.

This is the miracle of miracles, that the Son of God should be content to be a baby, lying in a woman's arms; the miracle of miracles which makes miracles possible in our demented world and our anxiety-ridden lives; the only event of real hopefulness in the history of the world or in the midst of our own despair. But, if the event is to bring about the miracle for us, then we too must make the journey to Bethlehem. We think we can do that now by switching on television, but that kind of second hand journey is of no use. We must make the journey for ourselves and that is a harder thing.

Every Muslim, once in a lifetime, tries to make the pilgrimage to Mecca. From Kano in Northern Nigeria, which is West Africa, millions of Muslim pilgrims make the long eighteen-month journey on foot to Mecca — a hard journey across Chad and the Sudan, with some dying on the way.

But we must make a harder journey. We have to lay aside our pride and sophistication, and walk in the footsteps of simple shepherds and wise men from the east, and with them we must be ready to turn aside at the Inn and to enter at the lowly door of the Stable, if we are to know that it is He. What a long way we have to come from the height of our pride, from the distance of our self-assurance and conceit!

But only if we make the journey will we find Christ. Only if we find Christ will we find forgiveness for our sins, meaning for all of life, and hope to illumine the darkness of death.

So let us go even unto Bethlehem, to see this thing which has come to pass which the Lord hath made known unto us, for unto us is born this day in the city of David, a Saviour which is Christ the Lord.

Do You Remember?

Do you remember the excitement of Christmas Eve when we ourselves were small? The solemn hanging up of stockings, the feeling of almost unbearable tension, the desperate attempt to keep awake that always failed?

Do you remember waking up on Christmas morning to the bulging stocking with its odd projecting shapes, and how cold we became running from room to room?

Do you remember when you had children of your own — creeping in to fill their stockings, their joy in the morning in the gifts they got and gave?

Do you remember the people who used to share our Christmas happiness with us and who have gone ahead? Do you remember — the Ghost of Christmas Past is never far away at this time of the year.

Do you remember?

Of course you do. But is that all that Christmas is — a kind of exercise in nostalgia? If it is, sooner or later it will fade. Other memories will overlay it and finally blot out these that have meant so much to us.

Once, in our town there were Trade Guilds and Cattle Markets and Horse Fairs. They had gone on for hundreds of years but they all shrank in significance and finally they ceased. So it would be with the Christmas story if all it is is a remembrance of the events of long ago. Unless it tells of a love still freely available, it doesn't really amount to anything, for it is this present which really matters. Unless the Christmas Gospel is relevant to Ulster and the Lebanon, to poverty and hunger, to looming terror in South Africa, and to our anxieties — unemployment, the mortgage, the teenage rebels, approaching age or nagging sorrow — it is not really relevant.

Is there any one answer to all of that? I think there is.

The answer — the only answer — is Love.

It is easy enough to love those who love us, for love begets love. But how are we to love the unlovely? How to love our enemies? How to love the undeserving, the unloveable?

We shall learn to do that only as we learn that we, the undeserving, the unloved, the unloveable, are loved by the eternal God. And that is the message of Christmas — that God loves each of us just as if we were worth loving, just as if there were no other to love. And that love is finally triumphant. The Christmas Story is only the beginning of the Gospel. It goes on to Calvary and to Easter morning where we see that the Love which came down at Christmas was finally victorious.

"Unto us a child is born. Unto us a son is given and the government shall be upon His shoulder and His name shall be called Wonderful, Counsellor, the Mighty God, the Everlasting Father, the Prince of Peace. Of the increase of His government and peace there shall be no end. They shall not hurt nor destroy in all my holy mountain, for the earth shall be full of the knowledge of God as the waters cover the sea."

That is why Christmas is as relevant today as it was 2000 years ago and why it will be relevant to the end of time. That is why it is as relevant to the old as to the young, to the sad as to the glad, to the rich and to the poor. For nothing that happens to us can finally destroy us if we know, really know, that God loves us and loves us for ever, and finally that nothing, not even death itself, can withstand that love.

That is why it is not only good tidings I bring, but the best tidings the world has ever heard or ever could hear.

For I bring you good tidings of great joy which shall be to all people, for unto you is born this day a Saviour which is Christ the Lord.

Magic in the Air

By the time a man has reached a good old age, he has spent about 2000 hours standing in front of a mirror shaving — about three solid months. How long the other sex has spent in a similar posture it is impossible to calculate, but speaking for myself I can say that by the time one has got to middle life, one has grown pretty tired of seeing the same old face looking back at one from the mirror. Most of us would be quite happy to trade it in for a newer, more sporty model.

That, perhaps, is why we are so fond of the Fairy Godmother in the Pantomime, with her magic spells. It's great — a flash and a bang on the stage and the pumpkin becomes a coach, the rats a pair of fine horses, the mice two coachmen and Cinderella an exquisite Princess. Would that it could be so for us, but alas it can't. We are pretty well stuck with the face and figure which has become only too familiar to us over the years. The same is pretty well true of character. We'll probably go on being as lazy, as bad tempered, as greedy, as irritable as we've always been. Like Tennyson we sigh:

"And ah for the man to arise in me
That the man I am may cease to be."
But it just does not happen. What we have been, we are and

what we are, we shall more than likely always be.

Except, of course, on Christmas Day, for there is a magic then in the air and a supernatural spell which never fails to work — even for the Scroogiest of Scrooges. Of course, it doesn't last. Fine we know that before many hours it will be back to business as usual — back to the same old bickering and greed.

Christ will visit every home today and while He is here we'll be on our best behaviour, but once we think the Visitor has gone, we'll lose no time in dealing with those who have taken advantage of His presence to put something over on us.

That is how it has been every Christmas so far. But it is not how it is meant to be. The Son of God did not become man so that life could be transformed for one day out of the 365. Jesus came so that life, all of life, every day and in every way, might be different. And it can be, for Jesus has promised us nothing less than the power of Almighty God to bring about the change. The Son of God visited *and* redeemed His people.

The world is all wrong. Our nation is all wrong. But what is wrong is not politics or economics. What is wrong with the world is us. What is wrong will only be put right when you and I are put right. The only one who can work the magic is God. In Christ He has shown that He is willing and ready to do just that.

What Christ can do for us one day, He can do for us every day; what He can do for one person He can do for all. And so I say —

Unto you — and you — and all of you is born this day in the City of David — a Saviour which is Christ the Lord.

Let us now go even unto Bethlehem.

CHRISTMAS DAY

News of a Saviour

Luke 2.11-12 (RSV) "For to you is born a Saviour; you will find a babe lying in a manger."

I'm not going to talk for long, so let us be clear what we are talking about — not about a dear little baby who became a nice kind man. There are lots of dear little babies, more and more all the time, too many in some parts of the world, and happily lots of nice kind men, but we don't celebrate their birthday. There is no excuse for the fuss we make about Jesus' birthday unless we believe Him to be unique, the same yet quite different from all other babies; unless we believe that He came from a sphere beyond earth's failure and despair. At Christmas, to speak plainly, we are dealing with the supernatural, with the miraculous; we are dealing at Christmas with a power other and greater than ourselves. We are saying that the Eternal Word of God has been made flesh.

The Christmas Gospel is News — news of a Saviour.

Well, we'll buy that. God knows we need a Saviour badly enough. We're in a mess and we know it. The world is in a tangle, the country on the slippery slope and we ourselves so confused that we don't know where to turn. Yes, we'll buy a Saviour.

Where will we find Him? Strangely comes the answer — "You will find a babe lying in a manger". Here is a strange thing. Who said anything about a baby? We accepted the offer of a Saviour and then we're told to go and look for a baby in, of all strange places, a manger.

We would have been happy to look for a Saviour in a palace or in a university, in a stock exchange or a parliament building, among the eggheads of Oxbridge or the gnomes of Zurich or the pundits of Brussels. But the angels insist that if we are going to find our Saviour at all, we shall find Him in a manger in an inn. Only those as humble as the shepherds would credit that story.

But unless we learn humility from the shepherds, we'll never find the Saviour we so sorely need. Our pride and conceit, our self-seeking will have to go, along with our sophistication and our intellectual pride. Only when we are obedient enough to search for the stable, and humble enough to enter it, will we find the Babe, and only when we, great grown men and women, kneel before the Babe and learn of Him, will we know that we have found the Saviour — our Saviour — the Saviour of the World.

Surely it is worth while to imitate His humility who "Came from highest bliss, down to such a world as this".

"For to you is born a Saviour;
You will find a babe lying in a manger."

So let us now go even unto Bethlehem.

It Shall Not Pass Away

Luke 2.15 "It came to pass."
Matthew 24.35 "My word shall not pass away."

"It came to pass." It's an odd phrase which appears twice in the second chapter of Luke from which we read. It came-to-pass. It is true of most things. They come to pass. Joy comes — and passes — and sorrow. Success comes — and passes. Failure comes — and passes. What was depressing you a year ago or rejoicing your heart? Can you remember? I can't. The seasons come — and pass. If winter comes, can spring lie far ahead? Youth comes — and passes all too quickly. Life itself comes — and passes. When a Pope is enthroned, the procession is stopped from time to time and a piece of magnesium paper is burned. As it quickly flares up and goes out, four words are spoken — "Sic transit gloria mundi" — "So passes the glory of the world."

Passing away is written in the world and all the world contains.

I can remember, as a little boy, the panic I felt as Christmas Day, so long awaited, wore on towards evening, knowing that when it ended, then there would be the great, yawning gap till another Christmas came.

It came to pass.

I wonder if what brings so many of us here, year after year, to bring in Christmas, is the wistful hope that here we may be in touch with that which does *not* pass, that here is something permanent in the midst of so much impermanence.

The walls of this ancient church have watched 760 Christmasses come and go. When they looked down on the first Christmas service here, bullock carts would be passing up the High Street. Later there would be horse drawn vehicles. The church, unchanged, has seen the coming of steam and then of diesel. Before television, before radio, before the telephone, before electricity, before gas, before clocks and watches, this building stood just as it is now. The same Christmas Gospel has been read 760 times.

Today, this church is more used than ever before. Why has it not long since been turned into a museum? Is it not because it stands as symbol of something far more permanent than itself, as symbol of the Eternal Word of God made flesh for us and our salvation?

Today's parties will pass and today's jollity; today's food and feasting. The Christmas tree will be placed with the rubbish and the decorations will be put away till next year. The things which seem important to us now will pass — our reputations, our bank accounts, our possessions, our furniture, our books, our houses. Even this Cathedral which has stood for so many centuries will one day crumble.

As Christ once said, "Heaven and earth shall pass away but my word shall not pass away." God's word to us in Christ is a word of everlasting pity and everlasting hope, of everlasting love and everlasting life which shall not pass away.

That is the good news I bring. That there is a God, a God who cares enough to come in Christ to save us all, and to save us for ever. If here and now in the quietness, you are aware not only of those sitting beside you and of the great and lovely church, but of something else — of someone else, a Presence unseen but real — then this Christmas need not pass when the parties end. If we here and now feel the nearness of the God who came in the Babe of Bethlehem, who lived and died and rose again, if we know that he is near, Christmas need not pass for us with the end of the day or the end of the year, or ever.

The Christ who was humble enough to come to the stable of an inn all those years ago, is willing to come into your heart, into your life, into your home, and to bring with him the sanity, the cleanness, the faith, the hope, the love he brought at first.

May Christ be with you now. May Christ be with you wherever you may go this Christmas Day. May He be an unseen guest at your table and be with you at your fireside.

May Christ be with you in all the days that are to be, in your joys and no less in your sorrows, in youth and middle life and age.

May Christ be with you when life itself is passing, and when it is past, may you be with him for ever.

It came to pass

Jesus said, "My word shall not pass away."

The Fear That Banishes Fear

Luke 2.10 "Fear not."

It is a curious thing that the two words of the text appear four separate and distinct times in the Christmas story. It is thus that the angel of the Lord greets Zacharias. Thus too does the angel address Mary and Joseph and, as out text records, these are the first words spoken to the shepherds by the lone angel who preceded the heavenly host on Christmas morning. How odd that so many needed reassurance at such a time! There is nothing very frightening in the coming of a little baby, one might think. Had it been a host of demons whose arrival was being intimated, or an alien army, flood, fire or earthquake, one could have understood the terror, but nobody is afraid of a newborn child.

We are certainly not afraid at Christmas nowadays. Some of the less sophisticated children may still have moments of awe and wonder, not entirely free of fear, on Christmas Eve or at the pantomime. Their eyes may widen when the tree lights are switched on or when they see their first "Santa Claus" of the season. But we grown-ups know better. Even the Christmas ghost just makes us smile. The angels on the tree are made of plastic and have been used, we know, for a dozen years or more. We have seen pictures of the other side of the moon and of the farthest planets. Sober scientists speak of the conquest of the universe. How could sudden dread fill our hearts?

Yet, underneath the gaiety, our lavish spending, our know-all attitude to the vastness of space and its secrets, we are afraid. We are afraid in the West of the vast numbers and vast power of Russia and China, afraid of the terrible weapons we have made, afraid of an unpredictable economy we cannot seem to control. As individuals we are afraid — afraid of illness, of missing the appointment we had hoped for, afraid of our relationship with people we love going wrong, afraid of growing old or lonely or ugly, afraid of dread, inescapable death, and, after it of "stepping out onto nothing". Like steam under pressure, our fear grows all the time, just because we will not admit it — cannot, indeed, will not, admit it. If once we did, the dungeon would be unlocked, and all sorts of unspeakable monsters would stalk abroad. Always the uncomfortable knowledge is with us that they are there. While we are making polite conversation over the teacups, we are forever listening for the crashing sounds of their breaking forth, fancying that we hear the echoes of their maniacal laughter. When we fall asleep they take advantage, and have at us in our dreams. And all this shows in the stress diseases that afflict us — coronaries, duodenal ulcers and the rest — and in our consumption of tranquillisers.

Perhaps our situation is not very different after all from the poor shepherds on the Galilean hills. They were afraid too — afraid of the Romans, of wild beasts, of robbers, of poor prices for their animals, and of ill health. What was it that swept all their fears away in the twinkling of an eye? The angel's "Fear not"? Hardly! Before the angel spoke a word, they had forgotten all about Romans, robbers, prices and pains. All their lesser fears, even their fear of death, had been swallowed up in the one strong, clean fear of God. The glory of the Lord shining round them, which had banished all else from their minds, engulfed them, so to speak, in the one overwhelming awe of the holy. It was not the fear of darkness which was troubling them now. It was the greater fear of light. Their road from fear to fearfulness was through the greatest fear of all. It was not to their worldly anxieties the angel spoke. They had all gone. It was to all that was left in their hearts — fear of the Lord.

Why our generation is so hag-ridden by terrors, why half the population can only face the world when fortified by drink and drugs, is because we have forgotten the fear of the Lord which is the beginning of wisdom and peace. Flee from God and myriads of devilish things pursue you. Turn to face God and all the demons flee, leaving only the awe of God. Once we know this, know of a surety that real felicity can be found in God alone, then the dread of losing Him will banish all other dreads and the joy of finding Him make pale all other joys.

It was to this mingled joy and dread that the angel spoke on the first Christmas. "Fear not — for unto you is born — a saviour, which is Christ the Lord." When they heard that, and had verified that it was all true, then the shepherds returned, glorifying and praising God. What had changed them? It was not that the price of wool had risen in the course of the night. Robbers still threatened, and wolves still lurked in the hills. The Roman yoke had not mysteriously been broken. The coming of the Saviour was not to turn stones into bread, nor to deliver the kingdoms of the world into the hands of saints. In some ways the shepherds had the same fears they always had, but now these fears were different, for they were seen in the perspective of the fear of the Lord and His love.

If with awe and wonder, in fear and trembling we make the journey this Christmas that the shepherds made, the love which casts out fear will enter into and possess our hearts, and we shall return to face the problems of the world, of the Church and of our own lives, no longer afraid; assured now that we have God-with-us, Emmanuel. Surely this is a Gospel worth making known to our fear-crazed world.

> "Trust in the Lord, for ever trust,
> And banish all your fears."

For He has shown how utterly we may trust Him by giving His Son to be our Saviour.

FIRST SUNDAY AFTER CHRISTMAS

The Shepherds Returned

Luke 2.20 "The shepherds returned glorifying and praising God for what they had seen and heard."

Have you ever been struck with the difference between going somewhere and coming back, between the outward journey and the return? Perhaps the reason why a return ticket used to cost less than two singles was that the return journey is worth a lot less. See the ladies setting off for a day at the sales — fresh and bright and chatty, taking an interest in everything. Meet them off the evening train — jaded and tired, very often silent, busy with their own thoughts of what the day has held. During the war, when large Naval ships were going to sea, the brasses were shining, the signal flags fluttering, the marine band playing, the sailors lined up on the deck. They came back battle-scarred, salt encrusted and dirty.

There are quite a few instances of return journeys in the Bible. The Children of Israel went to Egypt to better themselves, sure of a welcome. They came back with the marks of slavery on them, wearying for the homeland. The prodigal son left home, a young blade, with lots of money in his pocket. He came back in rags, half starved, ashamed. And, of course, the shepherds came in haste to find the Babe. After they had paid their respects to the Christ Child, the shepherds — returned.

This is the stage we are at in these days after Christmas. This has been called "Steak Pie Sunday". The feast of Christmas is past, and so there is a steak pie — all right in its way, but a sore climb-down from turkey or roast beef. We are all changing down into a lower gear after the excitement and wonder of Christmas. Already the bills have come tumbling in, the presents have lost their freshness and the darkness seems all the greater for the star that shone so brightly for a little time.

Well, if it is hard for us to get back to the routine of work or to school, how much harder for the shepherds to return after the wonderful things they had witnessed. They had been caught up in the greatest event the world has ever known. How could they go back to picking brambles out of a fleece, or hunting for ticks or righting a couped ewe? Nowadays the Sunday papers would have been after them for their story. They would have been interviewed on TV. Even in those days they could have tried to keep the excitement going, but they were too wise for that. Their job was waiting for them and so they returned to it without reluctance or regret.

And so must we. If our worship of the Christ Child has been genuine, we shall return to our work — our ordinary, daily work, and our week by week service — more eager to do it well, more gentle in our dealings with others, our faithfulness to the vision showing in all we do and say and are.

For, of course, although the shepherds returned to the same job, with the same difficulties, the same drudgeries, the same dangers, the same boredoms, they themselves were different. They returned glorifying and praising God for what they had seen and heard. From the beginning, those who sought out Christ returned from their journey, not weary and reluctant, but with a new vision of the worthwhileness of their work, a new kindliness in their dealings with their fellows.

This is how you can tell if you have really worshipped God at Christmas — not by any thrill you have experienced, but by what happens in the days to come.

It is love alone that can save the world — not your love nor mine, but the mighty Love of God that came into the world in the Baby born at Bethlehem. If we want it and are humble enough to receive it, that love will come increasingly into our hearts and lives, and through us find entry into a world that is literally dying for it.

That is the true glory and hopefulness of Christmas. This is our privilege and responsibility as Christians. Only so will we be like the shepherds who returned to their ordinary lives and their ordinary work, "glorifying and praising God for what they had seen and heard".

God is not a Baby

Luke 2.40 "The child grew."
Walking through the churchyard, I've often thought it odd that tombstones should record the exact date of birth of the person concerned. Does it matter so much? It would be more interesting if they recorded that the person was a good violinist or a splendid cook or loved the open air. After all, one may play a central role in one's birth but it is largely an unconscious role and not a very distinguished one at that. A mother may remember every detail but no one else does. I do not know on what day of the week I was born nor at what hour nor who was present. Far more interesting than the details of one's birth are events later in life over which one has somewhat more control and of which one is at least conscious! In the biographies of great men and women, the exact circumstances of their birth rarely merit more than a line or two, if that.

The birth of Jesus was, of course, the most remarkable there has ever been. The stories of angels, shepherds and wise men, with the humble couple for whom there was no room at the inn, have seized the imagination of men and women in every age. Nativity scenes can be found in every High Street and in thousands of churches; the young parents and the Christ Child have been depicted by all the great artists and the same picture appears on millions of Christmas cards. Nor is it surprising that an event so unique as the coming of God into the world as a little child should have excited the wondering gladness of people in every age and of every level of culture.

Yet the circumstances of the birth of Jesus are mentioned in only four out of the two hundred and sixty chapters of the New Testament. How extraordinary therefore that in recent years the celebration of the birth of Jesus has grown in importance as almost to overshadow all the rest of the New Testament. And the birth is made much of by those who pay scant attention to His life and teaching and death and rising for the rest of the year.

Sometimes one hears of the Christmas music from Handel's *Messiah* being performed in isolation from the rest of that majestic work. But that is surely improper. "He was despised and rejected" and "I know that my Redeemer liveth" belong along with "Unto us a Child is born".

Christianity is a package deal. You can't pick out the bits you like and leave the rest like some over-fed child at a party tea. Birth, life, teachings, death, rising, coming victory belong together. The one makes no sense without the others. We have to remember that the Child grew. We do not worship a baby god.

A baby is the most lovesome thing in the world, but a baby whose growth and development are halted is a sad and pathetic being. The word "baby", however caressing when applied to a little child, is an insult when applied to a grown man or woman.

Part of the humanity which Christ shared with us was that He grew in wisdom and stature. He said His first word. He took His first step. He cut His first tooth. "The Child grew" — and we must grow with Him. Our religion must not be a continual looking back to the days of our own childhood, nor to the wonderful thing that happened in Bethlehem. Christianity does not consist of the constant re-telling of an old, old story. It is a venturing forth in new and exciting ways in the obedience of God.

The year ahead will have its difficulties and challenges for us all. We can face them confident and unafraid, sure that Christ has His own plans for our world and nation and for each one of us. But we shall not find out what those plans are by a constant harking back to the circumstances of Christ's birth. The theology of the Infant Room will not suffice for our adult world. Of course, in all humility we must start with the Christ Child, but we must remember that the Child grew, and be ready to grow with Him.

It is not all over now that 25th December is past. If it really happened, it has only just begun. Christ came, not to pay a brief baby call on the earth and then leave it for ever. He came to visit and to redeem His people, and before He left, He promised that He would be with us to the end of the age.

If Christ really came to you yesterday, He will not leave you today or tomorrow. He will not leave you comfortless on the darkest day which may be ahead of you. He will come to you and finally will take you to Himself, that where He is, you may be also.

It is a wonderful Gospel and it is a complete Gospel, covering the needs of the whole world and covering all our needs in this world and in the world to come.

Herod did not succeed in his murderous intent to kill Christ as a baby. Blessedly "the Child grew" — and we must grow with Him.

LAST SUNDAY OF THE OLD YEAR

The Locusts Have Eaten

Joel 2.25 "I will restore to you the years that the locust hath eaten."

Locusts are near enough like crickets, reddish brown in colour with gauzy wings. They appear in the Middle East from time to time in such numbers as sometimes to shut out the sun and turn the atmosphere raw and dirty. Sometimes they come in successive waves for days at a time and when they have gone, not so much as a single blade of grass remains. Roads, fields, gardens, houses are covered with them and then left bare as the desert. The bark of trees is consumed. Hay, straw, leather, they eat everything that comes before them. The nicknames for the locust in Hebrew are "Shearer", "Swarmer", "Lapper", "Devourer".

A great plague of locusts had come to the land in the time of the prophet Joel, who sees the visitation as a reminder to the people that they are poor creatures at best, and as a summons to them to return to God in penitence.

"Turn ye even unto me with all your heart, and with fasting, and with weeping, and with mourning. And rend your heart and not your garments, and turn unto the Lord your God, for he is gracious and merciful."

If the people do turn to God there is no limit to God's kindness. He will drive off the plague and pastures will spring in the wilderness, the tree will bear her fruit and the figtree and the vine their strength. Then comes the gracious promise, "I will restore to you the years that the locust hath eaten."

Of course, in a sense God could do nothing of the kind, What the locusts had eat, they had eaten. What they had laid waste was waste — the hunger which had come to man and

34

beast in their wake would not quickly be forgotten. Just as we remember the year of the bad harvest, of the short corn, of the great frost, so the year when the plague of locusts made food scarce would be recalled for long.

But no pestilence lasts for ever, nor any famine. Sooner or later the locusts always pass, and painfully the farms and fields begin to recover.

Joel must have seen it happen often, of course. First the plague leaving the land desolate — a change of wind and the pests disappear overnight. A few showers of rain and vegetation begins to appear, and before long the land is fertile once again.

Even in our stern northern land it happens — a hillside burnt black in the autumn, covered again with heather in the spring and purple by the autumn. Who would believe that under the snow and frost, snowdrops are thrusting and the winter wheat germinating? Nature has marvellous recuperative powers and can often absorb and use the worst that we can do in the way of pollution. I remember well a hideous dump full of old mattresses, cans, rubbish of every kind, which has become a green playing field. The good earth in our ancient churchyards has absorbed the bones of our ancestors and remained wholesome.

So bye and bye the remembrance of the years that the locust had eaten would fade as men enjoyed the fertility of the land. "I will restore to you the years that the locust hath eaten."

The application of all this to the last service of worship in the old year hardly needs to be made. As we look back on the year that is passing and on the years that have passed, we are apt to have a sense of hopeless panic. We had hoped to accomplish so much and have accomplished so little. Each year passes more swiftly than the last and each year's end leaves us dis-satisfied and forlorn. We've had so many losses and disappointments, made so many mistakes, are conscious of so many failures, our days taken up with trivialities, knocking life out to keep life in — up, down, up, down, one day more, one day less. The locusts have eaten our years.

We cannot turn back the clock nor retrace our steps.

"The moving finger writes and having writ moves on,
Nor all your piety nor wit shall lure it back
To cancel half a line, nor all your tears
Wash out a word of it."

Very soon this year will be over, filed away with the years, unchanged and unchangeable. No matter how great our regrets, how deep our penitence, we cannot change the past. We can't eat our cake and have it. We can't live our years and have them again.

And yet, and yet. Creatures of time though we are, we have an escape route to eternity. Do you remember Browning?

"What's time.
Now is for dogs and apes
Man has forever."

The past is not completely past, for it is not complete in itself. It is a fragment, part of a larger whole which includes the present and the future. The nature of the past will not be known until the present and the future are added to it. When an artist starts to work, it is difficult to see at first what it is he is going to draw. So the nature of the past will be changed by what we do now and in the days to come, the final picture will be fair and good if we leave ourselves in the hands of God who alone knows what He plans. What survives for us from the past is part of ourselves, but what that past shall be and mean is determined by the whole, by the end — so long as God's grace is at work in us and for us, nothing is ever quite done with.

God from the rich stores of his eternity can easily make up and more than make up to us the years that the locusts have eaten. He who broke from Eternity into Time, by the same act, opened a door for us to escape from time into His eternity.

Although *we* cannot recover the lost years, nor rub out our mistakes, God can. Just as He changed the tragedy of the Cross into the triumph of the Resurrection, so He can change the tragedy of our squandered lives and lost opportunities into the triumph of the forgiven life of service.

"I will restore to you the years that the locust hath eaten." The meaning of that for us is just the forgiveness of sins — the central miracle of our faith. The forgiveness of sins is not God letting us off lightly. It is God taking the burden of our guilt on His heart of love and so bringing good out of evil, wisdom from our errors and strength from our weakness. It means that God is ready to take over responsibility for all we have done or failed to do in the past, so long only as we are prepared to start afresh with Him now, and give Him obedience in this present, and by His grace, in all time to come.

This history of our world and of our own lives is heavy with the judgement of God, but it is full too of His mercy.

"Tho' His arm be strong to smite
'Tis also strong to save."

It is not yet too late for us to recognise that we are living in a day of the judgement of God — a day when He has judged and found wanting and condemned a way of life which leaves no place for Him. If we recognise the judgement of God for what it is and turn to Him in penitence and faith, he will take away the signs of His wrath and show us signs of His abounding grace.

If, as we cast a glance backwards over the year which is passing, it moves us to penitence, then we shall be able to face the new year with a new resolve to obey His blessed will, which can hold no hurt for us or ours. We shall find then that God will use even our mistakes and follies of the past for our own good and His own glory. We shall find as Joel found that God is gracious and merciful, slow to anger and of great kindness, find in our own experience the truth of His promise

"I will restore you to the years that the locust hath eaten, and ye shall know that I am the Lord your God and none else."

FIRST SUNDAY IN THE NEW YEAR

How Are You Feeling?

Are you feeling fine this morning, confident, happy, full of enthusiasm, vigour and health, looking forward with calm optimism to 19—. Well if you are, I'm not! I've had a cold off and on for weeks and I'm tired of it. My desk is piled high with stuff I can't seem to get down to. There are quite a few problems looming to which I can see no solution.

So if you are feeling strong and jolly, just ignore me for the next few minutes. I'll talk to myself and (I suspect) to a good few people who are like me. It hasn't been an easy winter so far, and to cheer us as we face 19— we have prophets of gloom aplenty. Even some politicians are vying with each other to tell us how much worse things are going to be — more inflation, still unemployment, cutbacks in all sorts of services, the drug and alcohol problem increasing and no sign of peace in Ireland or the Lebanon. A great many people are having a struggle to make ends meet with heavy mortgages and higher prices. A great number of others are chronically under par healthwise. Some are fighting temptation of one kind or another, trying to hide from the world their heartbreak, disappointment or despair.

Whatever the cause, I'm perfectly sure there are a great many people near the end of their tether, just getting by and not sure how long they can carry on.

Yesterday I was at the New Year's Day performance of Handel's *Messiah*. The whole performance was splendid, but perhaps the most moving moment was the perceptible second or two of utter silence there was in the huge audience after the singing of one particular aria. "Come unto Him all ye that labour and are heavy laden, and He will give you rest" touched a chord in every heart.

None of us should be ashamed to accept that invitation. It is one of the perfectly legitimate purposes of religion to give rest and refreshment. We are not ashamed to go to bed at night to seek rest for our weary bodies. We should not be ashamed to seek rest for our weary souls. It is sometimes said critically that religion is the opiate of the people. That was first said, not by Marx, but by a churchman, Charles Kingsley, and it is perfectly true. It is an opiate, and there is a place for opiates. Not many of us get through life without them, and we are very glad to have them when we are in pain. Religion is a much safer opiate for the wounded spirit than some which are prescribed.

Of course it is not only that, but it *is* that. You ought to find relief here for the hurt of sorrow, for the bitterness of failure, the sourness of remorse, for what Browning calls "the pain of finite hearts that yearn". You ought to find rest here Sunday by Sunday in Christ. You will not find the whole truth here, for that is beyond the capacity of any human voice to speak or of any human mind to comprehend. You will not find a miraculous solution of all your difficulties, nor the healing of all your hurt, but you should find such rest as will enable you to face the work and worry of another week and the demands of those about you. Your burdens will not disappear as if by magic. Your responsibilities will not shift onto other shoulders, but if you ask for it you will get enough strength here — even if only just enough for the next lap of the race.

One of the oldest, wisest, kindliest members of the congregation was talking recently to a younger person who was questioning the usefulness of going to church. The old lady finished the conversation by saying in a downright manner "So far as I am concerned, I could not do without it."

Far better than tranquillisers, much less to be ashamed of than sedatives, is an hour of worship once a week, or a while each day spent with Christ. If it enables us to face our own difficulties with more courage, to do our own work with more faithfulness and to help others with more understanding we should not be apologetic about it.

"Come unto me, all ye that labour and are heavy laden, and I will give you rest."

And He will as no one else can.

But that is only part of the text. Without pausing for breath almost, Jesus went on to say what at first may seem a surprising thing.

"Come unto me, all ye that labour and are heavy laden, and I will give you rest. *Take my yoke upon you*."

It might seem that tired folk have enough to carry without the additional weight of Christ's yoke, however easy it may be. But the yoke which joins the strength of two oxen or two horses is not an extra weight. It is a sharing of the load.

As soon as we accept the yoke of Christ, we find we have Him by our side. The load which was too heavy for us by ourselves is shared by one who has never faltered or failed. There are countless men and women alive today who will bear witness that it is so. Day by day they are aware of a presence with them which strengthens and calms them, a comradeship that helps them and a hand that steadies them. "Live beside me", said Jesus, "and I shall teach you to be brave and kindly and serene. Whatever you have to face will be no worse than I had to face. Whatever you have to bear will be no heavier than the burden I bore, and I bore it alone. You need not do so for I am with you."

Coming to Christ is no timid, shameful escape from life. It is a facing up to it in all its challenge, peril and perplexity. "Take my yoke upon you", said Christ. "Take a share in my huge task of saving the world and you will find your own burdens lighter and your own work within your compass, for I shall be by your side."

We need not be the frightened, failing, defeated creatures of a day. We can and should be fellow labourers with God, yoke fellows with Christ, not skulking and sulking and fainting through life, terrified of each returning day, but rather moving from weakness to strength, finally by the grace of Christ to win.

By the great ends for which God made you, by His huge confidence in you and by the remorse you will one day feel if you choose any other meaner, more selfish way, I bid you for the world's good, for your neighbour's good and for the eternal good for your soul, accept the offer of Christ. Set out to live with Christ and to serve with Christ and to win with Christ — that having all things done and all your conflicts past, ye may o'ercome through Christ alone and stand complete at last.

"Come unto me, all ye that labour and are heavy laden, and I will give you rest. Take my yoke upon you, and learn of me; for I am meek and lowly in heart: and ye shall find rest unto your souls. For my yoke is easy, and my burden is light."

Landmarks

Proverbs 22.28 (RSV) "Remove not the ancient landmark which your fathers have set."

The Jews kept every seventh day as a day of complete rest — the Sabbath. Every seventh year they made a Sabbatical year and gave rest to their land, allowing it to lie fallow. The forty-ninth year, being seven times seven, they called the Year of Jubilee. In that year all Hebrew slaves were set free and every parcel of land bought in the previous forty-nine years had to be returned to its original owner.

These parcels of land had been marked off when Canaan was originally conquered. Each of the tribes was given a share of the land and within the tribes each family was given a certain area. These areas were marked off by distinctive stones or heaps of stones. The land given to a particular family could not be sold or given away, except temporarily. If it did pass into other hands, it had to be returned to the original owners at the Year of Jubilee.

Since the landmarks marked the bounds of what was in fact a perpetual possession of the family concerned, it was regarded as a very heinous crime to move a landmark so as to enlarge your own share of land at someone else's expense. It was, in fact, a kind of theft.

Hence the commandment in our text, "Remove not the ancient landmark which your fathers have set."

It is a commandment needed in every generation, not least our own. As we stand at the Gate of the Year, with so many uncertainties ahead of us, so many changes inevitable, it is important to keep the landmarks which our fathers have set.

It is true in a physical sense. Many people who came back to their old homes last week for Christmas and New Year, found a kind of comfort and re-assurance in the fact that this church stands where it did in a changing world. On the wider scene, the National Trust and the Government do a great service by preserving some of our heritage of fine buildings. If Edinburgh Castle and Westminster Abbey were to disappear, or some of our great houses were to be demolished, the lives of all of us would be poorer. They are part of our past and provide a standard by which our meaner building achievements can be measured. People from Australia and New Zealand, from America and Canada find a deep satisfaction in visiting our ancient cathedrals and castles, our battlegrounds and universities. They are all landmarks in our history and should be preserved.

So with less material things — the Monarchy, the home and family, marriage. Those who attack such things, who would substitute some elected official for the Queen and who despise marriage and the family as stuffy and suburban and stifling, are removing ancient landmarks which our fathers set for the best of good reasons.

Life is at times perplexing and at times we feel ourselves adrift in a turbulent sea. We need a few landmarks to guide us and those who shift those landmarks are flying in the face of the experience of the ages. The world did not begin when we were born. A long time before that, for us, very important happening, our fathers worked out the bounds within which life could best be lived and set up landmarks to prevent themselves and us from going astray. If there is some law which has stood for many generations, some custom observed through the centuries, some convention long obeyed, let us hesitate to tamper with what the ages have found to be useful and right.

On some matters the last word has been said about how life should be lived. Those mighty landmarks, the ten commandments, have stood the test of 4000 years and still stand. They need no argument to support them. Only disaster can come on those who trifle with them:

"You shall have no other gods before me.

You shall not make for yourself a graven image.

You shall not take the name of the Lord your God in vain.

Remember the Sabbath Day to keep it holy.

Honour your father and your mother.

You shall not kill.

You shall not commit adultery.

You shall not steal.

You shall not bear false witness.

You shall not covet."

These are not ten tests of which only five are to be attempted. They are not suggested courses of action to be considered nor experiments to be tried. They are moral and religious landmarks which we move at the peril of our own souls and of the fabric of our society. Given by God, they have been tested and tried by hundreds of generations. it is time we taught them to our young and began to do so by obeying them ourselves.

Wrong-headed as it may be in some ways, the movement called the Moral Majority in America is seeking after something important. I believe the great majority of people in this country want moral standards to be upheld and strengthened. The old simplicities of life, the stern morality of a past generation, were what made Scotland great and made Scots men and women respected throughout the world.

Of course, there were some things in the old world that had to go — there was prudery and dishonesty among the Victorians, although not nearly as much as is sometimes alleged. There was snobbery and some foolish social distinctions. But these did not belong to the basic standards by which our fathers lived. They were accretions and needed to be swept away. But let us beware lest we destroy the landmarks when we take down the spiked railings between them. Let us take the coverings off the legs of the grand piano by all means, but that does not mean that we should countenance the stripper!

But how to distinguish between the moral and religious landmarks, which must not be tampered with, and the purely passing conventions which are of no permanent significance? There is one single standard, unchanged and unchanging, by which all other standards may safely be judged. One landmark which has dominated and humbled and challenged and ennobled men and women for 2000 years — the life and teaching and death and rising of Jesus Christ. God has not changed at all, nor has the human heart, and God has met the heart's need in Jesus Christ.

Reject all else which your fathers found valuable, if you must, although so doing you will discard much of worth and value. But hold fast by Christ. To reject Him because of the forms in which men have sought to serve Him is madness — the madness that has brought our world, our nation to the verge of destruction. Let us beware lest in our contempt for the old we cut ourselves off from Him who said, "Heaven and earth shall pass away but my word shall not pass away." For no heart joined to His has failed to find peace. No life lived in His obedience but has had in it something of enduring worth and usefulness.

In all our enthusiasm for change, let us not remove this mighty landmark by which our fathers lived — the Cross of glory of our Lord Jesus Christ on which was laid bare the yearning love of the heart of God for all His children and for you and me.

"Remove not the ancient landmark which your fathers have set."

EPIPHANY

A New Creature in Christ

2 Corinthians 5.17 "If any man be in Christ, he is a new creature."

On New Year's Day the central heating in the Manse gave up about six in the evening, because the oil supply had frozen. We were quite philosophical about it. After all, we have one open fire. So we piled on the wood and dross and gathered round it. That was fine for fully five minutes. Then the chimney went on fire. We were not at the end of our resources. We have an electric fire — a bit old, but capable of giving a good heat, so we plugged it in. There was a flash like an atomic explosion and that was the end of that. It was almost a pleasure to have to go down to the railway station to see a son off on the 11pm train, but it was half an hour late and the station was perishingly cold.

There are times when we feel that everything is against us; when we feel like saying "Stop the world, I'm getting off"; when we feel that we cannot stand the place in which we live, the work we have to do or the people round about us.

When we feel like that about our world, we can do one of three things.

1. We can run away from it all, literally or metaphorically.

2. We can alter our world, our environment to suit us — or to suit us better.

or

3. We can hope for some alteration in ourselves to suit it better.

1. The first and most obvious thing to do if you don't like where you are is to go somewhere else. One recalls the famous advice of Old Bill in the shell hole, "If you know a better 'ole, go to it."

On this principle have acted those who made up the mighty mass migrations from Asia into Europe and down into Africa. In recent times Australia, New Zealand and Canada have been populated by people on the move, seeking a new life. "Go west, young man and grow with the country," the advice given in the United States of America by Horace Greeley, was expressive of the same urge.

Sometimes this urge to leave a disagreeable environment could not be satisfied in sheerly physical terms. For the slaves in America and the depressed classes in industrial England, the need to escape from an intolerable situation often took a religious form — Negro spirituals and hymns of pure escape like "In the sweet bye and bye", "There is a land of pure delight" and many others. In Psalm 55 we read "Fearfulness and trembling are come upon me, and horror hath overwhelmed me. And I said, Oh that I had wings like a dove! for then would I fly away, and be at rest." In times of cruel persecution or pain or in extreme age, we must sympathise with the desire to escape.

Yet this is a kind of doubt of God who does all things well and who has placed us where we are for His own good purposes.

2. A healthier reaction if we don't like our environment is to change it. From this has come all progress, all civilisation, all social legislation.

Men and women lived in Scotland before fire had been discovered, cowering in caves in the bitter cold, with no light through the winter nights. Even 150 years ago, city streets were practically unlit muddy filthy tracks, the churches unheated, no gas, no electricity, no ready-made clothes, exploitation of women and children in mines or factories, education hard to come by, travel only for the rich.

Man has greatly changed the environment, physical or social, in which he lives and must go on trying to do so. Yet each advance has brought problems. Advances in medicine have created the problem of the aged; control of plagues has created the problem of the population explosion. The very instruments of comfort threaten our health and peace — the motor car kills its thousands; the rising standard of living imposes greater and greater strain on those trying to keep up with the Joneses; the machines we have created, central heating and electric fires, have become our masters. In a country like Sweden, where poverty is almost non-existent, and medicine and social legislation are as far advanced as anywhere in the world, the rates for divorce and suicide and abortion are the highest in the world.

The more completely we change our environment to suit us, the more obvious it is that a changed environment is not enough. "The fault, dear Brutus, is not in our stars but in ourselves." The trouble is not out there, but in here, in our hearts. The difference between a happy person and a very unhappy one is not usually a difference of cause. More often it is a difference of temperament.

Wesley once visited a man living in the greatest luxury. As they talked, there was a puff of smoke from the fire. "You see," cried the man, "the sort of thing I've to put up with all the time."

If we are at odds with our neighbours, with our surroundings, with our world, the only adequate way of dealing with the situation is to deal with ourselves. But of course, that is the hardest thing of all to do. We can fly to the moon, instal dishwashers, videos, music centres and the rest, put up with a 1990 calendar instead of a 1989 one, but every morning you and I waken up face to face with the same old you and me, the same fears, the same greeds, the same jealousies and selfishness.

3. We can't change ourselves and it is just because we can't that the Gospel is Good News. It is news of a power not ourselves, making for righteousness, a power that *can* change us.

The newness we need is not far away in some distant land, it is not an alteration forced upon our world. It is in here, and Christ can bring it to pass. If we but live closer to Him and let Him have his way with our restless hearts, we shall find that His touch has not lost its ancient power, find ourselves braver, kinder, happier, more generous folk. "If any man be in Christ, he is a new creature."

It was for this that the Son of God came into the world. That mighty act of condescension was not designed to do some cosmetic work on an unchanged and unchanging wicked world. Christ did not come to patch up an old religion to garnish or embellish our overcrowded lives. He came to make all things new, to change us at the centre of our lives so that we no longer concentrate on self, but on Him.

It has happened — Saul of Tarsus, Augustine, Luther, Chalmers, Schweitzer — happened in such wise as to change not only these men, but the world in which they lived. It is happening to thousands today. It can happen here to you and me, if we claim the promise.

"If any man be in Christ, he is a new creature."

------------ · ------------

The Worldwide Gospel

Matthew 24.14 "this gospel . . . shall be preached in all the world."

The news of Christ's coming was at first known only to Mary and Joseph. Then to Elizabeth and Zacharias. Later it became known to the shepherds. All of these were Jews. Then came the Wise Men. We don't know much about them. We don't know their names nor where they came from — China perhaps or Iran. One thing we do know is that they were not Jews. They were Gentiles, and surely that was part of the design of

God, that from the very beginning the Good News of His Love made Flesh in Jesus Christ should not be confined to those of one race or colour. "This Gospel shall be preached in all the world." Again and again these words appear in the New Testament. "All people" was part of the song that greeted Christ's coming, and at the end of St Matthew's Gospel the command is given, "Go and make disciples of all nations."

This Gospel shall be preached in all the world.

It is gospel. It is good news. It is not a wise warning, it is not even good advice. It is good news.

When I call on people newly arrived in town, I sometimes get the impression that they think I have come to sell them something or to make some demand or even to utter some kind of threat. The fault may well be mine. What I ought to be doing is to give some good news.

Dr Robert Schuller, the respected American tele-evangelist, who has made such a spectacular success in his church in California, says that the whole content of his message is "God loves you and so do I." That is the essence of the Gospel, "God loves you and so do I", and in proof of His love God sent Jesus Christ, and in proof of *my* love I've come to tell you about Him.

Fundamentally, the Gospel is a statement of something that happened, not long long ago in Cloud Cuckoo Land, but nearly 2000 years ago in Bethlehem of Judea, when Augustus was Emperor and when Cyrenius was Governor of Syria. At that precise time and in that place, Jesus Christ was born. He lived and taught and healed and helped and died and rose again to show the love of God the Father to all His children. There is no threat there, no warning, no appeal, no demand. The Gospel is News — news of something that happened, which cannot be reversed and need not be repeated.

"This Gospel."

But if Jesus is quite clear that what He came to do was to bring good news, He is equally clear that that good news must be passed on. The Gospel must be preached.

Preaching is a curious activity, completely different from teaching or lecturing where what matters is what is taught, not who teaches it. It is perfectly possible to learn a foreign language by using cassettes. Once, in East Germany, I met a Russian lady, a Professor of English language and literature, who had never before spoken to an "English" person. But the Christian Gospel cannot be imparted impersonally. I'm not sure if it is helpful to have sermons printed or even preached on radio. They are essentially conveyed from person to person. The hearer knows the preacher. Ideally the preacher should know two things — the person to whom he is preaching and the Person he is preaching about — the human heart and the heart of God. His function is to bring these two together — the human heart in its need and the heart of God in its love, to bring them so close together that he himself no longer stands between.

What a task that is and what a privilege! No wonder Carlyle once asked, "Who having been called to be a preacher would stoop to be a king?" My old professor of preaching lies buried in a Highland churchyard. On his tombstone there is no mention of his honorary degrees or distinctions, but just this, "Arthur John Gossip, for 46 years a preacher of the Gospel" and what finer epitaph could there be?

Yet essentially and intensely personal though the preaching of the Gospel is, it was from the beginning intended to reach the ears of the whole world. Recently I heard it alleged by a religious affairs correspondent on radio that Christianity in India must be content to be one religion among many and that an unimportant one. It must be content to be nothing of the kind. Of course we must be courteous towards those of other religions or of none. But Christianity in India and everywhere else, if it is to remain Christian, can have as its objective nothing else and nothing less than the winning of the whole world. True there are only six or seven million Christians among the five hundred million of Indians. But if there were but one single solitary Christian, I would not doubt that all could finally be won. One person plus God is a majority in any land.

Sometimes we hear folk say of newcomers to an area, "They're not church people." *ALL* people are church people — actual or potential. My work will not be ended until every single soul in this Parish calls Christ Lord.

We are not told in the New Testament how many Wise Men came from the East with their gifts for the infant Jesus. There were three gifts but there may have been many more wise men. But, however many or however few, they were the first of many thousands of millions of Gentiles who have since made the pilgrimage to Bethlehem and have offered their gifts to Jesus Christ.

Mission is not an optional extra tacked on to the real work of the Church. It is its vital centre. The Church exists for mission as light is for shining or a fire for burning. We are Christians, not so as to hug to our breasts the assurance of our own salvation, nor even to drive ourselves to some kind of moral and spiritual improvement. We are Christians so as to spread the Christian faith which has come to us because others could not keep it to themselves, were driven by the same certainty that, "This gospel shall be preached in all the world"

"shall be preached" — the Gospel constantly re-interpreted and mediated through a human voice and a human life,

"in all the world" — the Gospel destined for every single living human being.

This is the content,
this is the strategy,
this is the aim of the Christian Gospel.

This is the obligation which rests on all who call themselves by the name of Christ. Here is the Charter of the Christian Church. Here is a command we dare not disobey or ignore.

"This gospel shall be preached in all the world."

WEEK OF PRAYER FOR CHRISTIAN UNITY

Christ Our Peace

Ephesians 2.14 "He is our peace."

Christ — our peace.

Peace for which countless blood-drenched generations have longed. Peace which still eludes us — mocked by the Lebanon, Ulster, San Salvador and by the vast stockpiles of fearful weapons in every land. Peace which is our world's most desperate need. How shall we achieve it?

It was said of Charles I that nothing became him in life so much as his manner of leaving it. When President Carter left the White House, he took leave of the American people and many felt that nothing in his presidency was so wise and dignified and statesmanlike as what he said in farewell to his fellow citizens. He rightly ignored the economic problems, pressing though they were, and concentrated on the absolute priority which must be given to peace. No matter how great our technological advances, no matter how marvellous our medical discoveries, no matter how complete our mastery of economic forces, all will be destroyed if war breaks out. No legacy that we can leave to our children and our grandchildren can begin to compare with peace. If we leave this legacy, all future generations will call us blessed. If we fail, if we permit nuclear war to break out, all future generations, if there are any, will call us accursed.

How is peace to be achieved? Not, I think, by arms reduction treaties, valuable though these are in themselves. If major war breaks out, it will only be a matter of time — and of a short time at that — before nuclear weapons will be manufactured and used. Our only hope is to avoid war completely and the

53

only way in which that can be done is by removing the causes
of war. The chief, if not the only, causes of war are the gross
inequalities between the haves and the have-nots. If these
inequalities are to be ironed out, considerable sacrifices will
be called for on the part of the rich nations — and that
certainly means us. Are we prepared to pay the price for
peace or are we prepared to contemplate nuclear war? There
is no third possibility. Are we prepared to accept a great
reduction in our standard of living? There is meantime
precious little sign of it. We are all so keen to maintain the
differentials between ourselves and others, so keen to use
whatever coercive power we have to get more and more for
ourselves, that the plight of those who have nothing seems
not to concern us. Every group seems to be trying to hold
every other group in the community to ransom and the rich
countries to hold the world to ransom.

How can this be changed — as it must be changed if the
horrors of war are to be avoided? It can be changed only if we,
you and I, men and women, can be changed. The causes of
war are not political or economic, they are moral. The
constitution of UNESCO stated "Since wars begin in the minds
of men, it is in the minds of men that the defence of peace
must be constituted."

I said the causes of war are moral, but behind morality is
religion. The hope of peace is finally religious. Arnold Toynbee,
the great historian, wrote quite soberly "For a true and lasting
peace, a religious revolution is a sine qua non". If we are not
ready for a religious revolution, we can make up our minds
for war. But is a religious revolution possible apart from Christ?
I think not. Christ, and Christ alone, can bring peace to our
souls, for Christ, and Christ alone, can bring us to God, and
away from God there is no peace for men and women, no
hope of change in thrawn human nature.

"Thou has made us for thyself, and our souls are restless
until they find their rest in thee." Christ is our peace.

But if we hope to be needed as peacemakers in the world, we must have peace in the Church and among the Churches. We must show that the thing works. This is the beginning of the Week of Prayer for Christian Unity and the way to Christian unity is the greater dedication to Christ of us all.

Let me take an anology from quite another sphere. Divorces in Scotland now number almost exactly one in three of all marriages. Part of the reason — although not the whole reason — for the sad figure is, I feel, the determination of most young couples nowadays not to have even one baby until they have been married for some years. The reason often given is that they want to enjoy each other's company for a time without the intrusion of a third person. I'm sure they are making a mistake. A new baby does not divide the mother and father. Quite the opposite. Their love of the same little being deepens and strengthens their love for each other.

So as we who call ourselves by the name of Christ are constrained by His love to love Him, we shall learn to love each other. So long as we try to look at each other, we shall only see systems of government and customs we dislike, and draw further apart. We have different traditions and histories. Nothing can alter or reconcile that which is past. Archbishop Laud and his service book was, and so ever will be, the enemy of the Covenanters. The only thing which will bring the Churches, despite differences of worship and government, to the unity which is the will of God, is if all Christian folk draw nearer to Christ. The closer we are to Him, the nearer we shall find ourselves to one another.

So peace in the Church, like peace in the world, can come only from peace in our souls and that peace only Christ can give.

An old writer said that when Christ made His will, He committed His soul to God, His body to Joseph to be decently interred. His clothes fell to the soldiers, His Mother was left to the care of John, but what should He leave to His poor disciples? He had no gold or silver but He left something of infinitely greater value — His peace.

"Peace is my parting gift to you," He said, "My own peace, such as the world cannot give. Set your troubled hearts at rest, and banish your fears."

Accept the legacy of Christ. Receive His peace into your own souls. Let it reign in your homes. Be at peace with your neighbours of every denomination or of none. Be a focus of peace in the Church and in the world so far as you can reach out and touch it,

"And the peace of God, which passeth all understanding, shall keep your hearts and minds through Christ Jesus."

———————— · ————————

LENT

The Thick Darkness — and God

Exodus 20.21 (RSV) "Moses drew near to the thick darkness — where God was."

Moses described himself as being slow of speech and of slow tongue, but there was nothing timid about him. It must have taken considerable courage to draw near to the great black mountain with the fog swirling about it, the lightning flashing and the thunder echoing from peak to peak. It was too much for the people. They were having none of it. Goodness knows, they would say, what terrors were curtained by the mist. The people stood afar off and, as they watched, Moses advanced alone and then, to their horror, disappeared into the thick darkness. And in the thick darkness Moses — found God.

That is a most surprising statement if you think of it. At the very beginning of the Bible, in the first chapter of Genesis, it is recorded that when God created the heaven and the earth, darkness was upon the face of the deep. And God said, "Let there be light", and God saw the light that it was good.

"Light", Milton said, "is the prime work of God." Throughout the Bible light is seen as being good and darkness evil. The Psalmist prayed, "O send out thy light and thy truth. Let them lead me. Let them bring me unto thy holy hill."

Our Lord Himself said, "I am the light of the world. He that follows me shall not walk in darkness but shall have the light of life." In the 21st chapter of Revelation it is said of the Holy City that it has "no need of sun or moon to shine upon it, for the glory of God is its light, and its lamp is the Lamb." How astonishing therefore that Moses found that it was in the thick darkness that God was.

57

Astonishing? I wonder. Some here may have found God in the sunshine of unclouded happiness, but far more have found Him when alone they entered the thick darkness. There is a certain shyness about God. He is not the companion for a pleasant walk on a summer day, or, if He is as near us then as at other times, our eyes are apt to be dazzled by the garish day and our wills ruled by pride. More likely it is in the valley of the shadow that we are most aware of the presence and the power of God.

"Even though I walk through the valley of the shadow of death, I fear no evil, for thou art with me, thy rod and thy staff, they comfort me." The valley of the shadow of death does not mean, or does not only mean death itself. It means any experience of deep depression or despair.

Which one of us could claim to have had no such experience? Even the saints — perhaps most of all the saints — know of a dark night of the soul, a time when life seems flat and profitless, religion an illusion, and faith a mockery, and God unreal. It can come because of some terrible experience — serious illness, alienation from some loved one, desertion by someone whom we trust, unemployment, the dashing of some long cherished hopes. Or it may simply happen — a cloud comes over the sun — and one is seized by a mood of deep melancholy.

However it happens, it is a desolating experience.

It is at such a time, when we are stripped of everything trivial and superficial, when we have no appetite for the pleasures and delights of life, it is then in the thick darkness, when our feet had almost slipped — that God comes.

Faith, real faith in the real God, does not come easily. It comes when we see that the only alternative is despair, the thick darkness — where God is.

The commonest cause of despair is sorrow, and it is an experience which comes to us all. No day passes from dawn to sunset, but some heart breaks. However sunny we may be in nature, however cheerful in temperament, there comes the day when the one we love is taken, and nobody else can help us then save God alone. When Moses went into the thick darkness, the people stood far off, and one of the terrible things about the darkness of sorrow is the awful loneliness. People are kind but the fact is that the loved one is not there and nobody else can take their place. The only one who can speak to our need then is He who can say, "I am the resurrection and the life. He that believes in me, though he die, yet shall he live, and whoever lives and believes in me shall never die." If we hear that then, even although everybody else removes and stands far off, we shall find that in the thick darkness, God is near.

And if we have found God in the thick night of our own soul and in our sorrow, we shall not lose Him in the last darkness we may none of us avoid.

Dying is lonely work and there is nothing in the Bible to encourage us to take a jaunty or casual view of it. Christ wept at the tomb of Lazarus. It is a great thing to have loved ones near, to have a hand to hold at the last, but finally we must walk into the dark river one by one — alone unless by then we have found that God is in the thick darkness. If we have, the darkness will have no terrors for us, for it will be lit by the presence of God.

So was it on the day when darkness was over all the earth, until from the Cross there came the cry, "Father into thy hands I commit my spirit." More than at any other time or in any other place, in that thick darkness God was.

However we may recoil from the thick darkness of doubt or of sorrow or of death; however lonely we feel when compelled to face one of these dread experiences, we shall find that we are not alone, for just when human companionship fails, the presence of God will be all the more certain, and in His presence the darkness will shine as the noon day.

So when our turn comes, Christ will be there. Do not doubt it. For He has promised, "Lo, I am with you always, even unto the end."

There is nothing to fear. The darkest road with Christ is better than the brightest road without Him. As Clement of Alexandria once said, "Christ turns all out sunsets into dawns." In the thick darkness — God is.

---------- · ----------

Strength Through Sorrow

Matthew 5.4 (RSV) "Blessed are those who mourn, for they shall be comforted."
At first sight, that may seem a sombre text, suitable only for a funeral service. but it's wise to mend your sails in fine weather. Those to whom as yet no great sorrow has come can be thankful, but no one is exempt from grief for ever. No day draws on to evening but some heart breaks.

"Blessed are those who mourn, for they shall be comforted." This is one of those sayings of Jesus which is dangerously easy to say and desperately hard to understand. It slips off the preacher's tongue so smoothly, but what does it mean? All of us would do anything to avoid sorrow for ourselves, and we sympathise with others who have been brought into it. How then, "Happy are the sad"? At first sight that sounds the sheerest nonsense, and it *is* sheer nonsense if it means what it is often taken to mean, "Don't worry. Though you are sad now, it will soon pass." I don't think that that is true — not always. If it were true, it doesn't help the present pain. It has certainly nothing to do with Christianity.

Twice this week — as almost every week — people have said to me, "Why did God let him die?" One cannot treat that question lightly, nor can one answer it, but in all tenderness and with all reverence one may ask some other questions of those that mourn. Would it really help to know why at this precise moment the loved one had to die? What hurts, surely, is not the perplexity about why now, but the fact of separation. When a child goes to hospital, or a dear friend has to go abroad, we know the reason for the separation, but it still hurts. No matter when we are separated it still hurts. If we were asked to name a date and an hour for the person we love to die, what date would we choose? If with certainty we knew that everybody would die, say on his seventieth or eightieth birthday, would life be greatly happier? Would it not become a dreadful nightmare as the fateful day grew inescapably nearer?

Of course, God could have saved us sorrow, but only by denying us joy. Sorrow is the price we pay for the joy we've known. It's a high price, but surely not too high:

"Had we never loved sae kindly,
Had we never loved sae blindly,
Never met and never parted,
We had ne'er been broken hearted."

But which of us would choose not to love?

An old lady once said to me, "I am determined now to let neither joy nor sorrow affect me." If she succeeded, what a travesty of human life was hers. Not to have lived would be better than to have lived without joy and sorrow. The mystery of life is prior to and more important than the mystery of death, but the one implies the other. Sorrow is not some strange, unlooked-for accident that happens to some. It is part of the package deal of life. We cannot ask to be delivered from it without opting out of life completely. All we can ask for is to have the strength to bear it and that is precisely what is promised in the text, "Blessed are those who mourn, for they shall be comforted."

The word "comfort" comes from the same root as fortitude, fortress, fortify and the like. To comfort is not to give ease or pleasure, but to give strength. The Beatitude does *not* mean that the mourner's pain will diminish, but rather his or her strength will grow greater — greater not only to bear sorrow, but to face life in all its majesty and challenge with a new humility, a fresh gentleness, a truer sense of values, a deeper compassion. All this sorrow will do, if we allow it to do what it was meant to do — bring us nearer to God. If it doesn't, it will bring us to despair. For there is no strengthening, no insight, no safety face to face with death and its seeming finality, save in God alone. The panacea of work has only limited usefulness. Travel, pleasure, new surroundings, drugs do not really help. Our only hope for ourselves or for our beloved on the other side is in the knowledge of the heart of God which we find in Jesus Christ.

We should not speculate much about the life to come nor what it is like. God wants us to live in only one world at a time. When we do think of it, we should not think of it apart from Christ. Let us see the life to come in terms of His promise that where He is, there we shall also be in what He calls, with utter trust, "My Father's House". If we learn from Christ, then when the last mile comes here for our beloved or for ourselves, it will not find us alone nor in despair. The love that brought Christ through death to life will not leave us or ours unhelped. If thus we can learn from Him in our sorrow, if with Him we can learn one day to die, we shall at least begin to understand and to believe, "Blessed are those who mourn, for they shall be comforted."

---·---

Things Not Seen

Hebrews 11.7 (RSV) "By faith Noah, being warned by God concerning events as yet unseen, took heed and constructed an ark for the saving of his household."
Things — not seen — as yet.

Sometimes, as we listen to the radio or watch television or read the newspapers, we might well think that all that matters in life are the things which can be weighed and measured, seen, touched, tasted and handled, bought and sold: motor cars, petrol, whisky, beer and tobacco. No matter who is speaking, there is the same dreary concentration on things. What a nation of greedy girners we have become. Without any Russian scheming, without a shot being fired, atheistic materialism bids fair to take over our country.

Of course food and clothes and houses are important if you are hungry or naked or homeless, but only a few of us are any of those things, and to allow the search for more and more things to control our lives is madness. It is to allow the means of life to supplant life itself.

Deep down we know it is nonsense. We know that if our husband or wife or one of our children were kidnapped, and there was no other way, we would give everything we have — houses, money, lands, furniture — for the loved one's safe return. Why when we are not in such extremity do we so constantly place a greater value on things than on people, forgetting that a person's true worth is what is left when all possessions are taken away?

As the father of sons, I'm sometimes sorry for the father of the bride, when I see the worried wrinkles on his forehead. Food and drink, flowers and photographs, clothes and hired cars have become so costly, and yet, what it is all for is the unseen — the love in two human hearts.

The things that really count are the things not seen — as yet. They are the things that finally matter — faith, hope, love. This whole passage in Hebrews is devoted to the proof of it. It argues that the Really Great were those who were under the control and compulsion of that which they had not yet seen — Abraham, Isaac and Jacob, Joseph and Moses, Gideon, Jephtha, David and Samuel. They were all men of vision — seeing what other men could not see. All were obedient to the call of the Unseen and so they had been responsible, under God, for all the great advances their people had made. Typical was Noah, who, being warned of God of things not seen as yet, prepared an ark for the saving of his household.

His neighbours thought that Noah was daft, building a boat so far from the sea — and such a boat. They pointed to the cloudless sky and the parched earth and said, "Use your common sense, man, and give up this foolishness. Anybody can see there is no danger of a flood." But Noah went doggedly on, despite their taunts, and all because of things not seen as yet.

Of course, Noah saw some things. He saw the evil all round about him and knew that it must end. Because God is God, wickedness cannot last. It contains within it the seeds of its own destruction and decay. Morals so depraved, behaviour so shameless, a civilisation so decadent could not endure. He saw perhaps too that the cracked earth cried out for water as men's evil lives cried out for judgement. So the conviction grew on him that it would be by a flood that the end of all the wickedness would be brought about.

If we have eyes to see, we may be driven to the same conclusion about our civilisation — sexual licence, drunkenness, idleness, tolerance of unnatural vice, contempt for law and order have all come together in ages past and have all ended in the same way. "One by one", said Matthew Arnold, "One by one ancient civilisations have crumbled, and all for lack of righteousness." That Noah saw clearly enough.

But some things he did not, could not see, for they had not happened — yet. He had to build his boat before the rains began. He had to act in the present for a future that was yet to be. So, with not even a cloud on the horizon, he built steadily on.

So it has always been with men and women of vision from Columbus to Simpson, from Galileo to Lincoln, from David Livingstone to Madame Curie. Those whose pioneering work has marked the progress of the human race, have learned all they could learn from the past, have seen all there was to be seen, *and then* have gone on in quest of things not seen as yet. Every deliverance of the human race from ignorance, from slavery, from pain or fear, every advance, has been made by those ready to answer the call of the unknown and to explore the unexplored. They have advanced in the only way in which it is possible to advance, by going up to the limits of their past experience — and then beyond it.

Always in life it is the past that is lit. It is that which we know. Before us is darkness — the things not seen as yet. *Now* is the perilous moment between light and darkness in which we live, and from which we must move forward in faith into the darkness which lies ahead. Always leading us are men and women of faith with their eyes gazing into the future to the things not seen — as yet.

So surely with regard to the most important things of all — with regard to life and its meaning, and death and its mystery, and God. As we grow older, some things, some few things, become certain. I could not doubt the existence of God any more, nor the life to come, nor the presence of Christ in the Sacraments.

That leaves much uncertain or unknown. Why suffering? Why sorrow? Why mental defect? Why cancer? I do not know. There are a great number of matters about which we can know nothing or about which our knowledge is scant indeed. And we should not be ashamed to admit it. We are but plucking at the very edge of truth.

C. S. Lewis once said, "Life is the echo of a tune we have not yet heard, news from a country we have not yet visited, the scent of a flower we have not yet picked." "Here", said St Paul, "we see as in a glass darkly." Here we know in part and we should not be afraid or ashamed to say so. There are many things not seen as yet.

But because of what we do see, we can trust God about the things we don't see, sure that although we do not see *as yet*, we shall surely see bye and bye. When I find one little piece of the jigsaw of life and then another which fits, and then another, I know that somewhere the complete picture can be found. There cannot be a part unless there be a whole from which it came. There is in our knowledge limited, partial, imperfect though it be, the promise and the foretaste of the perfect knowledge that is to be.

If God is kind in the little that I see or know — in the beauty of a flower, a piece of music, the handclasp of a friend, the kiss of a child, I can be sure that in the things not seen as yet, He is in no way different. Above all, when in the gentleness and pity of Christ, I glimpse the glory of God, I am entitled to assume that beyond my earthbound understanding there are reaches upon reaches of the love of God. Jesus looked deeper into life and further into death than anyone. As He looked from the Cross into the darkest mystery of all — the mystery of innocent pain and death, He saw in the darkness a face He knew and cried out "Father."

I believe that when we awaken on the other side, the face we shall see will be in no way different.

We see some few things here, not much, but enough to live by and by the light of which to die. We shall see *all* yonder and shall see God face to face and then we shall be satisfied.

Meantime we must and we can live by the things — not seen as yet.

———————— · ————————

PASSION SUNDAY

The Cry of Dereliction

Psalm 22.1 (RSV) "My God, my God, why hast thou forsaken me?"

Mark 15.34 (RSV) "'Eloi, Eloi, lama sabachthani?' which means, 'My God, my God, why hast thou forsaken me?'"

This is Passion Sunday. The word Passion here does not mean strong emotion. It has more to do with the passive suffering of the hospital patient, or the compassion of his relatives or nurses, than with passion in our sense of the word. On this Sunday, Christian people are asked quite deliberately to think of the suffering and death of our Lord.

It is good that we should do so. The Cross has so largely become a mere symbol, a thing of gold or silver to hang as a charm at a girl's wrist, or to gleam between golden candlesticks on an ornate altar. We have forgotten what a truly terrible thing it was, what a ghastly, degrading form of execution. Nowhere do we come nearer to what the Cross really was, nearer to its stark and cruel reality, than in these words which the pain of it wrung from the bravest heart that ever beat. "My God, my God, why hast thou forsaken me?" The fact that they are given in the original language shows how unforgettably they rang in the ears of those who were present. "Eloi, Eloi, lama sabachthani?"

In these words we are confronted with the depth and darkness of pain and death and with the mystery that lies at the heart of our Redemption. There is no use trying to ignore the cry. These words *were* spoken by Christ. They would certainly never have been recorded if they had not. The fact that they have been preserved in all their haunting challenge to our too easy faith is proof of the Gospel's utter honesty.

And we must be as honest. If what Christ is saying is, "Don't trust God. Don't believe His promises. He'll let you down when the crunch comes", then we must heed His warning and make what shift we can to bear alone what must be borne till the sorry business comes somehow to its wretched end. We do Christ no honour by refusing to look at the implications of His words.

First of all note that, although there is agony, there is no atheism in the cry. The call is not in doubt of God or denial. It is a cry to God, to a God whom Jesus knew to be His Own — "*My* God, *my* God." If we could only follow Christ's example and in our extremity cry to God, even if in bitterness of heart, we would find help. We are so apt to think that we must be polite in our prayers. We need be nothing of the kind. Read the reproaches Job, or the Psalmist, threw at God. God is quite used to complaints, more used to complaints than compliments perhaps, and is ready to listen. After all, if my child is afraid in the darkness and feels himself deserted or forsaken, I would not want him to keep silence. I would much rather that he cried out, that I may run to help him. Even if he feels that I have been cruel or unfair, I would rather know of it. And Jesus told us that we could safely reason from our feelings for our children to how God feels for us. "If you then, bad as you are, know how to give your children what is good for them, how much more will your Heavenly Father." If we feel forsaken by God, we should not guiltily repress our feelings nor give way to despair. We should simply tell Him so — as Christ did. Maybe only then will we discover that though we did not know it, God was quite near all the time, like a parent listening at a child's bedroom door. He is there, so we should not hesitate to cry out, even if it is only to say, "My God, my God, why hast thou forsaken me?"

The words, of course, are the opening words of Psalm 22. Just as we often call Psalm 23, "The Lord's my shepherd," so it may be that Christ was using the opening words of this psalm to refer to the whole. And though Psalm 22 opens with the cry of dereliction, it moves on to a note of triumph: "The kingdom is the Lord's: and he is the governor among the nations." The Psalm, as it were, itself finds the answer to the question with which it opens. And so the question, "My God, my God, *why* hast Thou forsaken me?" implies that Jesus believed that, although not at the time obvious to Him in the completeness of His humanity, there was an explanation of why God had permitted His suffering.

What was the explanation? Why did Jesus have to die in such suffering that this cry was wrung from His heart? Can we, however diffidently and fearfully, guess at the answer to that question? Let us ask another. What is the worst experience that can come to a man? Is it pain? Or sorrow? Or loneliness? These are borne with dignity and quietness all the time. Every minister of religion is constantly humbled by the courage and cheerfulness of those he visits. There is no more completely convincing proof of the power of the Gospel than the way in which it actually works in countless lives daily. People are able to bear fearful burdens with the help of God. But what if there is no awareness of God? Is that not the worst experience open to men and women — to have to bear pain or sorrow or loss without any sense of the nearness or love of God? To cry out in anguish and to hear no reply? To reach out in the darkness for a hand to clasp and to find nothing there? This is the most terrible experience when even God becomes a stranger. And Jesus our Lord chose to share the worst. He chose to be tempted *in all points* like as we are, so that when, despairing, we cry out, we may know of a surety that he is no stranger to our experience, but can share it with us.

Human life and death run out into mystery. There are no pat or tidy explanations. A child looks up at grown-ups with a puzzled half smile, as if to ask, "My God, why am I like this?" for he is mentally handicapped. A motor car skids on a patch of ice and turns a healthy young girl into a dumb wreck —

"My God, *why*?" A mother of four lovely children takes her life, leaving no word of explanation. All their lives they will ask, "My God, why?" The person dying slowly of cancer, the child victim of neglect — verminous, starving and bruised — the parents of a teenager hooked on drugs, all cry, "My God, why?" How senseless it all seems, how meaningless, how purposeless, and the clearest example of all of the wicked cruelty of life was the death of Christ! The Cross raises the problem of evil in its sharpest, most bitter form. It does not answer it, not fully, but ere the long day ended Christ had taken the sterile suffering and, in the midst if His agony, had wrought it into the redemptive purpose of God. The cry of dereliction passed at last into the cry of triumph, "Father, into Thy hands I commend my spirit." And through the darkness of tragedy, like sun breaking through a chill winter fog, we see the God of Love, Sovereign in the midst.

Ah, still we shall often feel like crying, "My God, why?" and when we do, we do no wrong. But we shall cry in the assurance that there is One who hears and who, some day, will explain. Meantime he does not deny us the grace to bear what must be borne till the evening comes, nor deny us Christ to be the companion of our way — Christ who made Himself one with us at our most despairing when He cried,

"Eloi, Eloi, lama sabachthani?" — "My God, my God, why hast Thou forsaken me?"

———— · ————

Sackcloth Within

2 Kings 6.30 (NEB) "When he heard the woman's story, the king rent his clothes . . . and when the people looked, they saw that he had sackcloth underneath, next to his skin."
John 20.27-28 "Then said he [Jesus] to Thomas 'See my hands

— and my side' — Thomas answered and said unto him 'My Lord and my God'."

Children of a past generation were often encouraged to be diligent, by being told that there is "plenty of room at the top of the tree". Of course it is not true. There is plenty of room at the bottom. On the topmost twig, waving in the breeze, there is room at the most for one very agile little bird with a good head for heights.

So it is in life. There are many members of a society but only one President; many sailors in a ship but only one captain; many citizens in our country but only one Sovereign. Since this is so, those of us who make up the great majority are apt to look enviously at the one who has inherited or attained eminence. To comfort ourselves we say "Uneasy lies the head that wears the crown", but we sometimes feel we could bear the discomfort in return for having the advantages which rank or wealth confers. It must be fine to have all the petty details of life taken care of. Even in the times of stress and shortage, those at the top of the tree seem to do pretty well. So must have thought the citizens of Samaria during this terrible siege. As day followed dreary day, they would see the King of Israel passing by in his magnificent robes and think to themselves, "It's all right for him to say that we'll hold out. They'll not be hungry up at the Palace."

Then came a horrible bit of cannibalism. Two women entered into a pact to eat their children. When one kept her dreadful bargain, the other relented and hid her child. The first, crazed with hunter and envy and shame told the terrible story to the King. Shocked and appalled, the King rent his kingly garments. And the people looked and "saw that he had sackcloth underneath, next to his skin".

The sackcloth used by the Israelites for seasons of mourning and humiliation and for certain religious rites was not the brown burlap made out of the jute for the import of which Dundee is renowned. It was really more like haircloth and was indeed made from the hair of camels or mountain goats. I remember as a small boy sitting on my grandmother's sofa with odd hairs from its black cloth pricking the backs of my knees. It was this sort of thing that was worn by the Jews as a girdle next to their skins in times of sorrow or shame. It was this that the people saw on the King's body when he rent his robes.

Outwardly cheerful and calmly confident, he had been sharing his people's sorrows and distress by means of the constant reminder the haircloth gave. This is the fate of kings. We need not envy the great or grudge them their perquisites. They pay very heavily for them. As Carlyle said, "Every noble crown is, and for ever will be, a crown of thorns." If we look closely, every king, every captain of industry, every leader of men is wearing beneath his fine clothes "sackcloth within upon his flesh".

Of course it is not only the great who suffer in secret. What is true of them is true in some measure and degree of all the folk among whom we live". Let us be kind to one another", said Ian Maclaren, "for most folk are having a hard battle." Some of the most cheerful, most seemingly self-satisfied people, turn out to be the most deserving of pity once one comes to know them. It is a mistake to envy any man his lot. Most people try to put a good face on things, try to hide their pain and fear and heartache. But we should not assume that others are always what they seem. Are you and I?

Certainly, as the story of his haircloth girdle spread, the people of Samaria would realise that they had misjudged their King. Their envy would change to admiration and pity. They knew now that he shared their affliction, and they would be ashamed of their own complaining. They would know that there was a great man on the throne.

These are always the stigmata of true greatness — not glory or comfort, but pain and pity. Isaiah saw it clearly, saw that finally the greatest of all must suffer most of all. "He was despised, he shrank from the sight of men, tormented and humbled by suffering; we despised him, we held him of no account, a thing from which men turn away their eyes. Yet on himself he bore our sufferings, our torments he endured — he was pierced for our transgressions, tortured for our iniquities." Do you remember when it was that the Apostle Thomas ceased to be "the doubter"? His spiritual pilgrimage did not end until he saw the wounds of Christ. He had companied with Jesus for three long years. He had seen His works of healing — unconvinced. He had heard the incomparable preaching and teaching — but still had been uncertain. He was not *sure* till at last Christ stood before him and showed him the wounds in His hands and side. It was this that shamed and humbled Thomas and won his heart.

And our hearts would be won too, and we would be humbler, less covetous, more loyal to Christ our King, if we lived near enough to Him to see the wounds which were the price of Him making Himself One with us. The Son of God is no distant spectator of our woes. He shared our lot. So He deserves not the grudging obedience of our wills but the loyalty and love of our hearts.

The King rent his clothes — when the people looked, they saw that he had sackcloth underneath, next to his skin. Jesus said to Thomas, "See my hands — and my side". Thomas answered and said "My Lord and my God".

———————— · ————————

The Cloister, the Crowd or the Cross

John 17.15 (NEB) "I pray thee, not to take them out of the world, but to keep them from — evil."

There is a tiny village in the South of Scotland called Borgue. It is not on the way from anywhere to anywhere. It has not been developed nor improved. It is just as charming as it has always been — a handful of houses, a church, a little school, a post office, a filling station and one small hotel. There is a saying in the surrounding countryside, "Out of the world and into Borgue." These days, with the world as it is — wars and rumours of wars, starvation in so many places and rampant materialism at home, increasing prices, plummetting morals, soaring crimes — we all feel at times like getting out of the world and into anywhere that is away from it all.

Some people, in fact, do opt out of our complex industrial society and either find some way of earning a bare living "far from the madding crowd's ignoble strife" or simply drop out of society altogether.

Holidays provide a temporary respite for most of us — a short-term escape from the pressures of life. but as we listen to the news or confront the difficulties of our own individual lives, we are sometimes tempted to go on holiday and not come back, to ask the world to stop for a minute while we step off.

Of course, it is not new. The Psalmist often expresses the feeling of being pushed by the pressures of life to the verge of despair. "Oh, that I had wings like a dove," he cried in one place, "for then would I fly away and be at rest" — a text familiar to us, set to Mendelsshon's lovely melody, "O for the wings, for the wings of a dove. Far away, far away would I rove."

If sometimes we feel like that for ourselves, we cannot but feel it even more for our children or grandchildren. We are all afraid of what this wicked world may do to them. It is not that they are worse than those of previous generations, but they are being exposed to temptations far more fierce and terrible than those which confronted us. When a Paedophilic Society dedicated to the corruption of children could, some years ago, advertise a meeting in London, things have touched a new low. The statistics for drug-taking, teenage alcoholism, crime and promiscuity make frightening reading for any parent. Watching our children grow, we cannot help but wonder if there is any way whereby we can get them away from it all, out of the moral, even physical danger in which they will stand when they leave home. Before we try to protect them from the impact of the world and its temptations — and discover how impossible it is — let us think for a little while about this prayer of Our Lord's,

"I pray thee, not to take them out of the world, but to keep them from— evil."

Christ was no starry-eyed simpleton. He knew what was in the heart of man. He had been brought up in Nazareth, the wickedness of which was a by-word. "Can any good thing come out of Nazareth?" men asked. Christ knew the world and, just before He died, He took a long look at it — at the great world of the decadent and corrupt Roman Empire, where vice had become almost a religion and sins were flaunted in a way which had no parallel till our own day. Christ saw the kind of test to which His followers would be subjected — the arena with the wild beasts, tortures, crucifixion and the steady, relentless pressure of a worldly paganism.

Then, having looked at the world in which they would have to live, Christ looked at the disciples — a pathetic handful of unsophisticated, untried men, confused still in their beliefs, quarrelling among themselves, the prey to all sorts of silly ambitions. Having looked, Christ prayed, "I pray thee, not to take them out of the world, but to keep them from evil."

One might have expected Him to pray that God would take this little band out of the world. Christ Himself could have told them to get away from it all, to flee to the desert to save their souls. In every age this temptation has confronted the Christian and many have yielded to it — the Cloister Temptation — to leave the world to go its own wicked way to the devil and to retreat either physically or at least mentally to some safe place where temptation cannot reach. Such were the hermits of a by-gone age. Such are some of the extreme sects of our own day, who isolate themselves so far as they can from all contact with the bad, bad world.

Whatever authority these earnest souls can claim for such a withdrawal, they cannot claim the authority of Christ — nor His example. He did not live a life remote from the haunts of men. He lived in the world. He had to, for it was the world He came to save and He loved it for all its folly and its sin. "God so loved the world, that He gave his only begotten son." "Go into all the world," Christ bade His disciples. The way of the Cloister is not the way of Christ.

But if we resist the Cloister Temptation, another at once besets us — the Temptation to be One of the Crowd, to become indistinguishable from anybody else, to join the queue for more money and more things, more pleasure, more food, more drink, to get our trotters into the swine trough. Most of us hate to be offensive. We like to be liked, and the world never lets up its pressure on us to conform. It is hard not to yield. It is easy to try to show that there's nothing of the Cloister about us and waken up to discover that there's precious little of the Christian either. When there is nothing to distinguish Christians from others, they are no longer Christians and are no use to Christ or to the world. If the salt has lost its savour, it is fit for nothing but to be cast out and trodden underfoot. Christian people ought to be different. Mr Pliable made little progress on the Pilgrim Way.

If the Cloister is no solution, neither is the Crowd.

There is a harder way than either and that is to live in the midst of the world by the standards of the Holy God. That was the way Christ lived and it brought Him to a Cross. Not the Cloister; not the Crowd; but the Cross. Neither to contract out, nor to compromise, but to live in the very midst of this most worldly world by the standards Christ has set. That will always mean self-denial and self-sacrifice and pain. In Christ's army every soldier is wounded.

If God had not wanted us to live in the world, He would not have placed us here. If He had not wanted us to be any different from others, He would not have come in Christ to die. The world is God's world, but there is evil in it — gaunt, cruel and bestial, such things as ought not to be in God's world. Just for this very reason, we cannot, must not try to get away from it to some place of safety for our own souls. We must get into the world, immerse ourselves in its needs and problems and face its evil in the power of Christ, sure that in the end we shall win.

As we see our children grow up and go from us into this perilous world, it will be with assurance, as well as with concern and compassion that we echo Christ's prayer for ourselves, as for them, "I pray thee, not to take them out of the world, but to keep them from evil."

PALM SUNDAY

Glory — God's or Man's?

Luke 19.38 "Glory in the highest."

"There's glory to you!" said Humpty Dumpty in *Alice Through the Looking Glass*. "I don't know what you mean by glory," said Alice, and most of us would agree with her, for all the frequency with which the word is found inside and outside the Bible. One meaning of it is fairly clear. It is what Shakespeare calls the "bubble reputation". It is an honour given to the successful soldier, to the victorious king, the elusive thing for which the athlete competes, and the scholar studies, the recognition by our fellows of our pre-eminence. It is that which attends the successful wielder of the will to power.

But there is another meaning quite distinct from this. There is a glory about a new-born baby — a kind of aura which surrounds the tiny thing:

> "Our birth is but a sleep and a forgetting:
> The Soul that rises with us, our life's Star,
> Hath had elsewhere its setting,
> And cometh from afar;
> Not in entire forgetfulness,
> And not in utter nakedness,
> But trailing clouds of glory do we come
> From God, who is our home:
> Heaven lies about us in our infancy!"

There is a glory too, too, about a bride which does not all depend on the pretty frock or the flowers. There is a glory about a young mother. There is a glory about a job well done. As the Spiritual has it, "You've got to get a glory in the work you do." Lastly there is a glory in serene age. See a calm, wise old face, lit with kindliness and humour, from which everything mean and selfish has long ago departed. There, like the glow of the rising sun as yet unseen, we may glimpse, reflected, the nearing glories of heaven.

Now, in this second sense, glory depends not at all on strength or victory or popularity. It is independent of men. It is something which comes straight from God. The baby, the bride, the mother, the job well done, the face of age, there is a glory in these which man cannot give nor man take away. It is the reflection of God in the mirror of man. There is at least a trace in it of the same glory of the only begotten of the Father, which men saw in Jesus Christ.

On the confusion between the two conceptions of glory, the whole tragedy of Good Friday and all the pathos of Palm Sunday depend. The glory which the crowd wished to give to Jesus as He rode into Jerusalem was human glory, the glory of conquest and victory and popularity — the brittle, passing thing which Caesar, Alexander and Napoleon shared. The only glory that Christ sought was that of doing the Father's will. When the Cross loomed frighteningly, inescapably near, Jesus, John tells us, lifted up His eyes to heaven and said, "Father, the hour is come; glorify thy Son, that thy Son may also glorify thee." After that prayer, Christ was ready to glorify God by His humble submission to a cruel and shameful and despised death, and so to receive the glory from Him that never was on land or sea.

What a picture in black and white Palm Sunday represents! The poor peasant riding on an ass being hailed as a king; the life and movement of a procession drawing inexorably nearer to the blackness of Calvary; the joy of the disciples, so soon to be turned to sorrow; their attachment to Him so soon to become base denial; the palm branches so soon to be replaced by the bare dead wood of the Cross. All the shamefulness of man's glory is etched there in its garishness, and all the glory of God's shame in its simplicity; all the glory of man — his honours, his achievements, his wealth, his success, his popularity, his victories — so transient and tinny, so hollow and sham. "All flesh," quoted Peter, "is as grass, and all the glory of man as the flower of grass. The grass withereth, and the flower thereof falleth away." All the glory of God is there in the silent figure riding on a borrowed donkey into the city where He was to die.

How easily could Christ have become the leader of a popular revolt, He who spoke as never man spoke, to whom the common people flocked in eagerness! But it was long since He had seen the offer of the kingdoms of this world and the glory thereof as a temptation of the devil. He who works for glory from man must work to man's dictation and accept the terms of the crowd. He who seeks the glory of God must be ready to see the praises of the crowd turn to curses, to receive, not glory in the world, but shame. And Christ was ready. He had made His choice. He, who knew the hearts of all men, knew how brief His popularity would be, how quickly the fickle mob would turn and rend Him when His refusal to do their bidding was understood. Before he entered the city he had counted the cost. "O Jerusalem, Jerusalem, thou that killest the prophets, and stonest them which are sent unto thee, how often would I have gathered thy children together, even as a hen gathereth her chickens under her wings, and ye would not." Christ knew that for those to whom God's glory is all important, there is only one road — the stony road to Calvary.

The choice that He faced and made, is the choice with which each one of us, too, is confronted — the glory of God or the glory of man. But if, in any sense, we seek to follow Him who was born in a stable, who died on a cross and who lay in a borrowed tomb, the choice is made for us already. We shall choose — as He chose — the glory of God. That will mean that we shall lose the glory of man — reputation, riches, the plaudits of the crowd, but we shall have the glory that can never alter or decay — that of doing the Father's will. It carries with it all that is truly good and pure and loving, all that is of lasting and enduring worth. It is the supreme gift in life, making rich and adding no sorrow, and it carries with it the life everlasting.

As that — the glory of God — becomes our search and our hunger, we, too, shall begin to share the life of God, to be changed from glory into glory:

"Till in heaven we take our place,
Till we cast our crowns before Thee,
Lost in wonder, love and praise;"

and take our place in heaven amidst the discovered glories of the Lamb, echoing the song of the angels at the very first, and the cry of the Palm Sunday crowd —

"Glory to God in the highest!"

―――――――― · ――――――――

The Lord Has Need

Mark 11.3 (RSV) "The Lord has need of it."

Two events in the last few days of Christ's life He clearly planned with some care. One was the Last Supper in the Upper Room. the other was the ride into Jerusalem. The fact that the donkey was ready waiting, and that its owner let it go, shows that there must have been a previous agreement with the owner and that the password for the operation was "The Lord has need of it."

The events of Palm Sunday were not a chance happening, not a spontaneous demonstration. They represented Christ's solemn claim to be the Messiah. Not a Jew in Jerusalem but would know of Zechariah's prophecy, "Rejoice greatly, O daughter of Zion! Shout aloud, O daughter of Jerusalem! Lo, your King comes to you, humble and riding on an ass." Jesus our Lord had been humble, none ever humbler, mixing with the toughest, most vulgar of men and women without any trace of condescension; laying hands on leprous sores, sharing meals with the poorest. But now He was laying claim to be the promised one, the King of Glory, the Messiah, the Son of David.

So, in His choice of a phrase as password, He chose one indicating rather the command of a King than the appeal of a beggar. There is a certain note of authority in the phrase, which brooked no denial or delay. "The Lord has need of it."

1. "Lord."

Jesus, although willing to wash the disciples' feet, knew, even as He did so, who He was. "You call me teacher and Lord; and you are right, for so I am."

The most sacred institution of the Jews was the Sabbath — the sign of God's choice of them. Quite calmly, as if there could be no dispute about it, Jesus said, "The Son of Man is Lord even of the Sabbath."

In the Sermon on the Mount, with absolute authority, He says, "You have heard that it was said to the men of old — but I say to you."

No wonder His hearers said that he taught them as one who had authority, and not as one of their scribes.

This is something we need badly to remember. We are apt to speak of Christ as if He were a supplicant looking for our support. I hear people say, "I'll maybe come to church some Sunday," as if they were about to do a good turn to God. There is a story of a lady in Galloway, who when she was 102, declined the honour of a proposed visit to her home by King Edward VII. We regard that as strange, but we don't think it funny that people should decline to meet Christ or should say that they will meet Him when they take the notion.

Sometimes in church I feel I should shout, "Watch out! Be careful! You are dealing with Him with whom we have to do. He will come to be our judge. Our eternal destiny is at stake. It will be decided by Him, and by no other."

> "'Tis the Lord, O wondrous story,
> 'Tis the Lord, the King of Glory.
> At His feet we humbly fall,
> Crown Him, crown Him Lord of all."

2. Yet He is a strange Lord, too.

"The Lord has need."

We know what a Lord is — someone with power and wealth and privilege, whose whim is at once satisfied. But here was a Lord who could not pay for His own funeral, depended on a friend to look after His mother, and rode to His death on a borrowed donkey.

Other religions think of God as splendid, self-sufficient. "Nor wanting, nor wasting, Thou rulest in might" as our own hymn says. The Psalmist makes God say, "If I were hungry, I would not tell you; for the world and all that is in it is mine. Every beast of the forest is mine, the cattle on a thousand hills."

How silly to suggest that He by whom the worlds were made needed anything — far less the loan of a donkey. But thus Christ chose. He who, "though He was in the form of God, did not count equality with God a thing to be grasped, but emptied Himself, taking the form of a servant"; "though He was rich, yet for your sake He became poor"; knew hunger and thirst and weariness and poverty and temptation; has a feeling for our infirmities.

Most of us are conscious of need as we stand before God. We are ashamed and in need of pardon; afraid and in need of help; perplexed and in need of light. We put a good face on it. We are jolly and at ease. But underneath we are all anxious and needy. We need not be ashamed, for the Lord, the King of Glory, has need.

"The Lord has need."

3. "of it."

The villager would be delighted to lend his donkey. No doubt he wished he could have offered an elephant or a camel or even a horse. But Christ wanted nothing other than that which the disciple could offer, and He's still the same.

He needs us all, rich or poor, young or old, educated or not, talkative or silent. Jesus has something for us all to do — some kindness to inject into His world, someone to keep from despair, some routine job to be done faithfully and well to his glory.

Don't hold back because of false pride or a false humility. Christ who has given Himself for us is entitled to claim whatever we can give, of service to our fellows, or help to the Church, of love to Himself. We have no right to hold anything back from Him who held nothing back from us. We can be sure that He won't reject us or what we offer, who, of a little donkey, said,

"The Lord has need of it."

GOOD FRIDAY

His Mother

John 19.25 "There stood by the cross of Jesus his mother."

There is, under God, no other person so important to us as our mothers. Through them we receive the gift of life itself and in the early years, which we now know to be of decisive importance, nobody begins to equal our mothers in the extent of their influence upon us.

Since our Lord Jesus Christ was truly and fully human — a man — it follows that, humanly speaking, one of the most important people in His life was Mary. A lot of harm has been done by exaggerated doctrines about Mary, getting very near to worship. She has been called "the Mother of God" — a phrase without meaning. But a lot of harm has been done too by a tendency to forget all about her. After all, she was the woman chosen by God to be our Savour's mother, and as such she deserves, not worship of course, but honour. In a sense she stands for all humanity.

She alone had been with Him from the beginning and was with Him right to the end. She had made her mistakes about her Son, had been cross with Him for arguing with the learned men in the Temple when he was only a lad, had tried to get Him to retire into obscurity and avoid all the trouble, had even wondered if He had lost His reason. But through it all she had remained His mother, and now, when the end was coming — "There stood by the cross of Jesus his mother."

No sadder sentence has ever been written. We are always apt to feel that it is wrong for children to die before their parents. Before the Battle of Bothwell Bridge, the Covenanting leader prayed, "Lord, spare the green and tak' the ripe." There is nothing more heartbreaking than a mother's loss of a son. to

85

have given a boy birth with pain; to have brought him up with care and love; to have watched him grow to manhood; to have prayed for him and hoped for him; and then to have him die before your eyes must be agony indeed. When the Son was such a Son as Jesus, when He died such a death as He died, the pathos and horror of the scene beggars the imagination. Yet — "There stood by the cross of Jesus — his mother."

"Stood by Him" can mean a number of things. It can mean an innocent by-stander, one who is not really involved. Many such stood watching Christ die. Or it can mean to stand by waiting for orders. In a ship, before an order is rung up on an engine room telegraph, the "stand-by" is given so that the engineers will be on the alert. There would be some such at the Cross, waiting for they knew not what — Nicodemus perhaps, or Gamaliel. But "stand by" can mean more than that. It can mean to give one's active support and help to someone when he needs it — to throw in one's lot with him. To have someone stand by when misfortune or ill-health or slander strikes, means everything.

There is no doubt in what sense Mary stood by the Cross. It was not idly nor even alert and ready for action, but as one who identified herself utterly with this wonderful man whom she had brought into the world. Mary was heartbroken but she was not ashamed. Of that I am sure, for otherwise she would not have waited to see her Son humiliated and crucified. The fact that this gentle peasant woman had not fled to sob out her agony alone but had stood by, shows that somehow she had known that this was not the end. Unashamed she took her place with her Son, defying the world and the world's judgements, content to abide God's time to see by what wondrous means He would give Christ the victory.

And now, my friends, what about us? We call ourselves by the name of Christ. We come to church. Are we just interested spectators of the great drama of Christ's birth, life and death and rising? Are we standing by, ready to begin our service, alert but not quite committed? Or are we prepared to take our place with Christ, and throw in our lot with Him?

In our day and age, the line is being drawn ever more clearly. It is for Christ or against. The world's need is desperate — and our country's and our city's. There is and there can be no neutrality. Either we must commit ourselves against Christ, or in trembling and fearfulness we must take our stand with the saints and prophets, martyrs and apostles of every age. But if and as you take your stand with Christ, remember that when she who loved Him best of all stood by the Cross of Christ, a sword seemed to pierce her own gentle heart.

Mary was no strange being not quite of this earth. She was a woman with perplexities as great and feelings as deep and a heart as easily wounded as any woman here, but with a loyal spirit which could not be daunted. And she challenges us to a loyalty like her own — at a like price — asks us to make common cause with her, pleads with us to dedicate ourselves with all the courage and sincerity and self-sacrifice within us, that we may not be ashamed when we remember that whatever the others may have done,

"There stood by the cross of Jesus his mother."

EASTER DAY

The Lord Has Risen

Luke 24.34 (NEB) "It is true: the Lord has risen; he has appeared to Simon."

The Lord has risen? True or false? If it is false, if death was the end of Christ, it will be the end of us and of those whom we love. If it is false, evil must triumph in the end, for death is the trump card of evil. If death triumphed over Christ, so did evil. If it triumphed over Him, it will certainly triumph over us and there is no sense or meaning in life, no hope for lost mankind, and I am wasting my time and yours.

But it is not false. It is true. The Lord has risen. That is what Easter is all about. It is not about the annual miracle of spring. It is not about Easter bunnies or bonnets, nor cakes, nor eggs. We are not talking about the well-nigh universal belief in some form of survival after death — immortality, re-incarnation, or what you will. We are not dealing with myths or fairy stories or fables to comfort the weak minded. We are dealing with an assertion made in or about the year AD 30 by eleven ordinary men — not gurus, nor mystics, nor holy men. Fishermen they were, and tax-gatherers and the like — men not given to childish fancies. Do you remember Mr Gradgrind, that eminently practical man in Dickens' *Hard Times*, who had no time for imagination or fancies, who dealt only in facts? These companions of Christ were somewhat of the same mind — a tax-gatherer who dealt in cash, fishermen who fought with wind and weather and nets and boats. What these hard headed men who were the companions of Christ asserted was that their Master, who had undoubtedly been killed, whom many had seen being buried, that that same Lord had undoubtedly risen from the dead, that they had seen Him and spoken with Him — alive.

This was the message of the first Christians, this the foundation on which the Church was built. This the foundation on which it still stands. And the continuance and growth of the Christian Church over twenty centuries is proof that the foundation is not flawed. The Lord is risen indeed.

Of course there are difficulties. There are no photographs of the Risen Christ. There are no television recordings. He made no appearances to His enemies, nor to strangers — only to friends, although on one occasion to over five hundred at once. There are apparent discrepancies with regard to the precise sequence of events, but on the fact that He was risen, all the disciples were agreed. This is what turned the handful of terrified followers into the most determined and successful band of missionaries the world has ever known. They were absolutely convinced that Jesus — the same Jesus whom they had seen die — had passed through death and emerged victorious on the other side. In the unequalled words of the Authorised Version, "Now is Christ risen from the dead and become the first fruits of them that slept." "O death, where is thy sting? O grave, where is thy victory? Thanks be to God, which giveth us the victory, through our Lord Jesus Christ."

The Lord has risen indeed. Let us rest ourselves on that.

Yet, if the Resurrection be a mere fact of history, something that happened long ago and is finished and done with, it cannot really matter to us. That Christ faced evil and sin and death and conquered them, may be interesting, but hardly relevant for us who quail before these things every day. Christ's victory matters only if it can help us to be victorious. So the Risen Christ of history must become the Risen Christ of my own experience.

I do not suggest that many of us will have visual experiences of Christ like the two on the road to Emmaus, or like the few at the lakeside in the morning light, or like the disciples in the upper room. He does not come to doubters among us to show His wounds, as He did to Thomas. But sometimes I have been sure that he was near. With a handful at an evening service, at a great communion or at a bed of death, I have known that Jesus lives. Moreover, when I talk with people, I find that if I try to defend the Church, I get into awful tangles. A discussion of the Bible can be of little help. But when I speak of Christ, people will listen and doubts are silenced and eyes are opened and hearts are comforted.

"All very subjective and personal", you say, but are not the subjective and personal things the things that matter — things like love and hope? And once a great number of subjective and personal things are added together, do they not amount to something more? When I like a given piece of music, it signifies little, except of course to me. When many millions are moved and quieted by the same piece of music, century after century, generation after generation, we know it has greatness within it. When I find that High Anglicans and Salvationists and Black Africans and American Baptists, having no previous contact with each other, tell in precisely the same words of their experiences of the Risen Christ, is it not obvious that they are in touch with reality, with the same Lord who spoke to the disciples in the upper room?

Moreover, the fact that He influences national and international affairs as no one else can, is proof of His importance not only for a handful of the pious, the mystical few, but for many. In every city of the world, in almost every street — in London and Beijing, in Belfast and San Salvador, as well as in New York and in Paris — the Easter Gospel will be read today and the bread broken and the cup of wine passed from hand to hand. Eleven hundred million people call Jesus "Lord". Because this is so, He has power to sway, not only isolated individuals, but races and nations. Look abroad in the world. Look to South America. In whom is there any hope save in the Risen Christ? What other free forces survived for so long in East Germany and Romania save the Church of Christ? Who else survived the enmity of Red China but the

Risen Christ? Is there anyone alive or dead who can begin to compare in sheer living power with Christ today?

Great conquerors come and go. Christ lives on. He is just as much risen, just as much alive, just as influential in today's world of drugs and silicon chips, as He ever was in Palestine. It is not only that Christ, then and there, rose from the dead long ago. He is risen. He is risen indeed.

"And has appeared to Simon." That, in the opinion of the disciples, was the most surprising thing of all: that, having risen from the dead, Christ should have chosen to appear to Simon — to Simon the braggart, to Simon the coward, to Simon who had denied Him thrice. And for the name "Simon", the names of countless billions of the wise and simple could be written in. For to them He is not only the Lord who rose nearly 2000 years ago, nor even the greatest personality in the life of the world. He is the Friend who companies with them from day to day speaking as no other can to their troubled hearts, as He spoke to the disciples long ago.

"It is true: the Lord has risen; and has appeared to Simon." If we are ready to receive Him, He will come to us too — not because of our faith or our worthiness, but simply because, like Simon, in our failure and doubt and fear and sorrow we need Him very much. Ah sure, we see as but through a glass darkly, the best and wisest of us, but we see Jesus, see Him clearly enough to know that one day we shall see Him as He is, see Him face to face and know Him as we are known. There, in the company our beloved, with the bleakness of our sorrow ended, we shall see Christ risen, ascended, victorious — see Him and at last be satisfied.

As you trust in the Lord who rose so long ago and as you live by the help of Christ who is risen, do not doubt that, when you finally come to Galilee, you will find Him waiting for you — as He said.

"It is true: the Lord has risen; he has appeared to Simon."

The Great 'If'

1 Corinthians 15.14 (NEB) "If Christ was not raised."

When politicians are interviewed on television, radio or at public meetings, they always say that they are eager to answer any questions put to them. It is easy to tell when a question is asked to which they don't know the answer. They begin their reply by saying, "Now that's a good question, a very good question." Then they go on to try and drown the awkward question in a flood of irrelevancies.

The Bible is an honest book, perhaps the most honest that was ever written. Far from dodging the awkward facts or the difficult questions, it thrusts them into the very forefront of our awareness. It says, "You sometimes wonder timidly if God cares. Listen to this." And we hear the Psalm which Jesus quoted on Calvary, "My God, my God, why hast thou forsaken me?" It says, "You are worried about the problem of the innocent suffering." It then takes the Cross, not an article of gold or silver or varnished wood, but a roughly hewn and knotted thing, brutal, ugly, with a Good Man nailed cruelly to it, and asks, "How's that for innocent suffering?" We all have our moods of doubt and despair — not least those of us in the ministry. So has the Bible. We do God no honour by pretending to a faith we do not have or have only spasmodically, or by asserting things we don't really believe.

Thomas, who spent three years constantly in the company of Christ, doubted right up to and beyond the crucifixion. Peter was so unsure of Christ that he denied three times that he even knew Him. Martin Luther once said, "I was driven to the very abyss of despair so that I wished I had never been born. Love God? I hated him."

Where Thomas and Peter and Luther doubted, we need not pretend to an assurance they were not given. So let us begin by admitting that it is hard to believe in the Resurrection. Aristotle said, "Death is terrible, for it is the end." We have all watched someone suffering from terminal illness gradually disintegrate and decay and then — death. It *looks* final enough. And Paul faces up to the possibility that it *is* final. "If Christ be not risen", he said, and we must face that question too.

What if Christ was not raised?

What if we have no hope of life after death?

What if we shall never see our beloved dead again?

What if there is no hope available for us?

What if we are fated to go down in the end before the mighty onrush of wickedness?

What if it is not true? What if the whole gallant history of the Christian Church is built on an illusion, on a hoax? What if the first Christians were torn by the lions and the later martyrs — Hus, Cranmer, Latimer, Ridley and Wishart — were burned at the stake for nothing? What if missionaries murdered in China and Africa in more recent days died for a silly mistake? They all died because they were sure that Christ died and rose again. What if Christ was not raised? There is nothing surer than this, that if Christ was not raised, nobody else will rise. What if there is nothing after death — just blackness and despair? What if the world is an accident? What if love be deception?

"Some little talk there was of thee and me,

And then no more of me — or thee."

If Christ was not raised, then the world will finally freeze or boil and life will cease and there will be nothing at the last, as there was at the beginning.

If Christ was not raised, then evil is stronger than good, and darkness is stronger than light, and death is stronger than life, and death will prevail.

Let it be admitted there are difficulties about the Resurrection. There are differences in the accounts given by the writers of the four gospels. Of course, the very fact that these differences are recorded is evidence for the fact that Jesus rose. Any policeman or judge knows that where the accounts of an incident given by several witnesses tally exactly, they are dealing with rogues. Honest men differ in their recollections of the simplest incident and the differences in the accounts of Matthew, Mark, Luke and John prove that they are honest.

Moreover, the mighty history of the Church is very convincing. Twelve frightened men somehow became the greatest missionary force the world has ever known. Something gave the disciples astonishing new life and hope. *They* were quite clear what that something was. It was that they each of them had seen and spoken with their risen Lord. The message they proclaimed was that Jesus, who had been crucified, was risen.

There it is then.

Against the Resurrection are some weighty arguments — our own experience of death, and common sense.

For the Resurrection are the evidence of the Bible and the history of the Church.

You weigh the evidence and you vote for or against.

If Christ was raised. If Christ was not raised. If that were all, most of us would give a verdict of "Don't know".

But that is *not* all.

I know that Christ rose from the dead, for I know that Christ lives. He has worked miracles and dead men work no miracles. Not long ago I visited a home where the father of the house was an alcoholic. I need not say "was". He is an alcoholic, but has ceased to drink and he is in no doubt that it was Christ — the living Christ — who wrought the miracle. He said to me, "Some people doubt if Christ turned water into wine. I can tell you that He turned whisky into a house, carpets and furniture for me, and that's a bigger miracle than turning water into wine."

One Easter Sunday evening years ago a group of youngsters, of whom I was one, were arguing about the Resurrection. All the while a dear old lady had been sitting quietly in the corner of the room. Finally she stood up and said, "You young people are clever and I'm not. I'm just a stupid old woman and I could not argue with you. But — I know my Saviour and I know He lives. Good night." And when she left the room not one of us was in any doubt.

If I know the risen Christ, I know he must have risen. If I do not know Christ as alive, as the Companion of my onward way, it does not matter to me whether he rose 2000 years ago or not. The Resurrection as a fact of scripture or of history avails nothing if it is not a fact of our experience. Unless and until I can say, "I know that my Redeemer liveth," I have no answer to the haunting doubt, "If Christ was not raised."

The Resurrection is not a theory to satisfy our curiosity about death, nor is it a fact only of history to be argued about by scholars. It is a fact of experience. "If Christ was not raised" That was not the end of the passage. *This* is how it ended:

"But the truth is, Christ was raised to life — the firstfruits of the harvest of the dead — O Death, where is your victory? O Death, where is your sting? God be praised, he gives us the victory through our Lord Jesus Christ — Therefore, my beloved brothers, stand firm and immovable, and work for the Lord always, work without limit, since you know that in the Lord your labour cannot be lost."

Since Christ is risen, all is worth while — finally, supremely, completely worth while. It is worth while to strive and, even if we fall, to rise and try again to be better men and women, truer, kinder, more brave and generous, more steadfast to resist temptation, more ready to serve our neighbours and the Church. The effort is worth while. The hope is not illusory.

If Christ was not raised.

But the truth is Christ *was* raised to life.

He is risen indeed.

I know that my Redeemer lives.

ASCENSIONTIDE

Why the Ascension?

Matthew 24.14 (NEB) "This gospel will be proclaimed throughout the earth."
Matthew 18.20 (NEB) "Where two or three have met together in my name, I am there among them."
Matthew 28.20 (NEB) "Be assured, I am with you always, to the end of time."

Ours is a materialistic age. We are dominated either by the theoretical materialism of the Communists or the practical materialism of the West. We all have a consuming interest with things we can touch and taste, manufacture, buy and sell. We are apt to conceive even of religion in materialistic terms — not as spiritual experience, nor as theological truth, but as practical service. What we mean by religion is best expressed in Christian Aid. At one time Christian people making their wills, bequeathed money to evangelistic enterprises or foreign missions. Now they are much more likely to remember social services like Eventide Homes. Perhaps the change in emphasis was overdue. But we do well to remember that all of these practical expressions of the Gospel came into existence because someone had a profound experience of the Unseen God. They all grew out of a supernatural religion.

To take an analogy, to a landsman it is always something of a miracle that a ship can find its way on a trackless ocean to the exact spot on the earth's surface for which it is making. there are no milestones, no signposts on the seas, no roads or roundabouts. The navigator finds his way, not by standing in the bow peering over the stem to where the ship cuts through the water. If he did, the ship would come to disaster and certainly never reach port. To make sure that it does reach its destination, he must continually check his position by the sun, the moon, the stars and the far horizon. So it is in religion. We shall steer the Church aright, and our individual courses, not by peering continually at what is directly in front of us, but by checking our position with the heavenlies, by gazing often at the far horizon.

So we need not apologise for turning our thoughts at least once a year to the Ascension of Christ. At first sight the story of the Ascension seems far removed from our experience. At one minute Christ was there with the disciples — recognisably the same person as had walked with them and talked with them during the three years of His ministry. At the next He was just not there. Even the disciples seem to have been puzzled, almost stunned by it. They stood gazing up at heaven until called to reality. Even afterwards they could give no very clear account of what had happened. Nor can we — and understandably. Jesus was passing from one sphere of life to another quite different, from our three dimensional world into a world in which dimensions have no relevance. You cannot weigh the weightless, nor measure the immeasurable, nor describe the appearance of someone shedding appearance — *dis*-appearing. All you can say is that it happened.

"Very well," it might be said, "let it be allowed that it happened and that it cannot be as described. Why did it have to happen?" The answer is, I think, that the Ascension had to happen so that Christ could keep the three promises of the text:

(1) "This gospel will be proclaimed throughout the earth."

(2) "Where two or three are met together in my name, I am there among them.

(3) "Be assured, I am with you always, to the end of time."

(1) "This gospel will be proclaimed to all nations." From the beginning Christ had been clear that he came, not to save a select few, nor even the whole nation of Israel, but quite literally to save the whole *world*. "The field" he said, "is the *world*." "I

am come that the *world* might be saved." "Go ye and teach all nations."

Up to the Ascension Christ had spoken to the few only, had left but a handful when he died, had appeared when he rose at the most to some hundreds of people. Now he was for all mankind. So he is still. The Church is incurably, unchangeably missionary. If at the moment the missionary impetus has been lost, it can be but for a time. True, there are no longer lands unexplored to which the Gospel can be taken with the white man's idea of civilisation. But Christ longs for the Chinese and the Indians and the peoples of Russia no less than He longs for the Africans, and they shall be His when He makes up His jewels. Christ ascended that His reign might extend over all the world, till the earth shall be full of the knowledge of God as the waters cover the sea. "This gospel will be proclaimed throughout the earth."

(2) Christ's second promise was, "Where two or three are met together in my name, I am there among them." The Ascension had to happen so that Christ should no longer be in one place only, but wherever His people gather. How impossible it would have been if the risen Christ had remained in Jerusalem. By and by the disciples would have died, but this haunting Presence would have remained. The eye of the whole world would have turned to this place — the roads, the seas, and now the air, crammed with those hoping to have experience of the risen Christ and knowing that nowhere else could he be met with, save in or near the Holy City.

I have never been in Palestine and sometimes have thought that I would like to go. But Christ is no nearer in Bethlehem, Nazareth, Capernaum or Jerusalem than he is in Dunblane, London or New York. He has promised and he keeps his promise: "Where two or three are met together in my name, I am there among them."

"This gospel will be proclaimed throughout the earth." Christ is not for the few, but for all.

"Where two or three are met together" — anywhere — "I am there among them" — Christ not for one place but for everywhere.

(3) Last, "Be assured, I am with you *always*, to the end of time" — Christ not for one time, but for ever.

People sometimes speak as if the Christian Church has had its innings, that it arose, that it flourished and now must die. It is true that the particular forms in which the Gospel is presented or embodied must change. There is nothing perpetual about Gregorian chants or Geneva gowns, nothing sacred about 11.15 and 6.30 as hours for the worship of God. The Church may adapt. Indeed, it *must* adapt to the changing circumstances in the life of men and women, just because Christ is not for an age, but for all time — and for eternity. Christ ascended, that He might be with his own to the end and that they might be with Him thereafter for ever.

Christ not for the few, but for all.

Christ not for one place, but for all the world.

We can believe that and pray for it and work for it, as we know that Christ is for you and me; and we can believe that, for we have His own sure word of promise that cannot be broken.

"Be assured, I am with you always, to the end of time." So He is and so He will be — for ever.

————————— · —————————

Think Big

Acts 1.11 (RSV) "Why do you stand looking into heaven?"

This is the Sunday after Ascension — the Sunday when we remember that the Risen Christ, having continued with the disciples for a while, was taken from them in a way that they knew to be final so far as this world was concerned.

The Ascension was not an accident. It was necessary so that Christianity might cease to be the local thing it was and become the universal thing Christ always knew it had to be. It had to happen so that the Gospel could be proclaimed to all people everywhere — not only in word but in deed also.

But the Ascension had another purpose — not only to direct the Gospel to all people on earth but to direct all people on earth to their final destiny in heaven. Christianity is irrevocably, inescapably other worldly. It sees man's destiny, not in terms of this world but of the world to come, not in terms of time but in terms of eternity. It declares that the humblest life cannot be described in terms of producing and consuming, but only in terms of God's august and majestic purpose that it should be lived with Him for ever.

Possibly the greatest danger of our age is not badness, but pettiness and triviality. Our days and our minds are filled with little things, with buying and selling, cooking and eating, with the superficialities of social life. Our reading is mostly of light literature, our entertainment slop. Unless we are brought up short by the death of a friend or some national tragedy, our thoughts, our words, our lives are all on the surface.

When did you last discuss anything with a friend but banalities? Some people never breathe deeply — they use only part of their lungs. There is a shallow breathing of the mind as well as of the lungs. We may drive our cars at top speed, but we rarely change our minds or our souls out of bottom gear. No wonder they become sooty and sluggish. I remember an oculist telling me why so many people need glasses — the eye is meant to focus now on something close, now on something in the middle distance, then on something far away. But in modern conditions we hardly ever look at anything more than a few yards away, and the muscles of the eye weary. Literally, we need far, far oftener to "Lift up our eyes to the hills". This was what was always distressing Christ. "I came," He said, "that they may have life, and have it abundantly." You are content with so little when you could have so much.

It is not a matter of our jobs. It does not matter whether we sail the seas or sell things, preach sermons or grow potatoes. What does matter is what our motive is for living. What fills our minds at our work? What are the topics of our conversation — food, clothes, the weather, other peoples' follies, our own petty triumphs? Or do we make room for the big things?

Think big. That doesn't mean, or shouldn't mean, be greedy or ambitious. It means fill your minds with big thoughts — not with spites and greeds, not with vanities and touchiness, not with the vulgarities of money or pleasure. Think big and talk big.

This is especially so in religion. This hour on a Sunday morning should open windows in the soul to the majestic themes of the greatness of God and the love of Christ and the need of the world. It is so easy to become trivial in our religion, to make much of denomination and forget the Kingdom, to fuss about vestments or no vestments, about committees and church furniture, about forms and orders of service, to become excited about buildings and forget about God. He and He alone is finally important, and our relationship to Him — and to one another.

And to one another. This we cannot forget in a world such as ours — it is not surely accidental that Ascensiontide and Christian Aid Week often fall in the same period. It is true that our relationship with each other is mostly at the level of the trivial. A wife's, a mother's love is not shown in profound statements nor in tender endearments, but mostly in terms of clothes washed and ironed, food well cooked and a house kept comfortable. The service that most of us give our fellow men and women is in equally unspectacular ways, doing our work, whatever it may be, faithfully and kindly and always letting our final purpose shine through. We show our discipleship, not by the kind of work we do, but by the way that we do it; by whether we do our work as a means of extracting as much money from the system as we can, or as the service of Christ in the service of our fellows. Big things are made up of little things and it is possible to make details serve great and good ends.

What more trivial, more vulgar, more commonplace than money. Yet it can be used for the noblest purposes and to serve the greatest ends. We should never be so heavenly minded as to be no earthly good.

If we need to be reminded, as Ascension does, that man cannot be understood in terms of this world alone, it is yet here that his duty lies. The better we know our Risen and Ascended Lord, the more He weans us from the vulgar and earthly, the more surely He will send us into the world with a new zest to serve, by what we give and by what we do and by what we are, our brothers and sisters of every race and class, for whom, as for us, He was ready to die.

"Why do you stand looking up into heaven?" This same Jesus, who went about doing good, who healed and helped and fed the hungry and washed the disciples' feet, this same Jesus is Him whom we meet in every frightened child, in every hungry, needy fellow man and woman. This same Jesus shall finally be our judge, and the basis of His judgement will be — as you did it, or did it not, to one of the least of these my brothers and sisters, you did it, or did it not, to me.

PENTECOST

Glory in the Tabernacle

Exodus 40.34 "The glory of the Lord filled the tabernacle."
Acts 2.4 "They were all filled with the Holy Ghost."

The Tabernacle was a sort of mobile church, a tent which the Israelites were commanded to pitch, whenever they made camp, in their forty-year long journey from Egypt to the Promised Land. I suppose that if they were to preserve their identity as a people whom God had delivered from slavery and for whom God had a wonderful destiny, there had to be a symbol of their faith. Otherwise they might quickly have degenerated into just another tribe of wandering Bedouin, believing they knew not what, with no sense of their high destiny. So they were told that wherever they settled in their wanderings, the Tabernacle — this tent — was to be set up.

They were given the most precise description of it and of its contents. It was to measure 45 feet by 15 feet. The walls were to be 15 feet high. The outermost court had to have ornaments of brass, the inner ornaments of silver, and the innermost Holy of Holies fittings of purest gold. The most elaborate directions were given for the setting up of the Tabernacle and for its conveyance from place to place. The Israelites followed all these instructions to the letter. What sacrifice it must have meant for this impoverished tribe to set aside so much of their wealth for their portable church, comparable perhaps to the sacrifice it must have entailed in the Middle Ages, for tiny cities to build the great Cathedrals of Britain, when the inhabitants were living in mud and wattle hovels along with their pigs and goats.

The Israelites do not seem to have complained about the expense. Perhaps they had a truer sense of values than we do,

103

who spend millions on sport, gambling, armaments and alcohol, travel and cars, and our pennies on God. The Israelites gave their best for the Highest.

At last all was ready — the altar in place and the seven-branched candlestick, the vessels of gold and the hangings of silk. The moment that they had waited for had come when they would discover if all their careful preparations were a waste of time and money, or not. If nothing happened now, the brass and silver, the acacia wood and the gold might just as well be scrapped.

There is a break in the narrative. The people had done all they had been asked to do. Would God accept their labour and sacrifice? There is a breathless pause. The cloud covered the Tent of the Covenant — *and then* — the glory of the Lord filled the Tabernacle.

On the first Pentecost, the birthday of the Christian Church, the disciples were assembled with one accord in one place — an undistinguished-looking little handful, waiting for they knew not what. Then the glory of the Lord came upon them and they were all filled with the Holy Ghost. So the Church was born.

"The Church". What does that mean to you? This building, or does it mean the General Assembly, or does it mean the Church leaders — the Archbishop of Canterbury, the Pope, the Head of the Salvation Army? Or does it mean the whole organisation and paraphernalia of religion — Baptism and the Lord's Supper, the Ministry, stained glass and organ music, bibles and hymn books, Sunday Schools and Youth Organisations, F.W.O. envelopes and covenants?

Well, let's not despise these things. Everything has to have some shape or form, some organisation. Every idea, every ideal, every purpose has to be embodied. One may rightly mistrust those who love mankind but cannot stand people, who believe in marriage but treat their wives abominably, and equally one can doubt the sincerity of those who believe in the Church, in

God, in Christ, but just can't find a congregation perfect enough to suit them. Everything has to be embodied and the embodiment will never be as perfect as the ideal which it embodies.

The Israelites needed the Tabernacle, the golden candlesticks, the Mercy Seat, the Ark of the Covenant, the symbols 4 of the greatness and holiness of God. In the same way, we need symbols, outward forms to express and embody the unseen things which finally are the only things that matter — the wedding ring, the flag, the bread and wine, the water of baptism.

But, just as the Tabernacle was nothing until the Glory of the Lord filled it, so the Church is nothing but sterile, lugubrious nonsense, except the Glory of the Lord be within it.

Of course the goatshair tent in the wilderness, with its bits of brass and silver and gold was a pathetically inadequate dwelling for Him whom the heaven and heaven of heavens cannot contain. Of course the most magnificent church that was ever built is almost laughably inadequate for the worship of the God of Gods, and of course all churches under heaven are subject to misuse and error. The minister is often obscure, the organisation is clumsy, the setting aesthetically unsatisfactory, but none of that matters if the Glory of the Lord is in the midst. If the Glory of the Lord is not there, the most sublime architecture and music, the most correct liturgy is worth nothing. And if the Glory of the Lord is to be revealed, it can only be at the pleasure and by the will of the Lord.

I have no doubt that Revival will come and that the tides of greed and lawlessness and sensuality will be swept back and a new love for things of God and the ways of God will seize the hearts of men and women. But the day will come, not by our contriving, but by the reappearing of the Glory of the Lord in the midst of us.

It has happened over and over again, often in the least likely of places. To the Covenanters amid the bleak, misty hills of the West of Scotland, to John Wesley in a London mission hall, to John Bunyan in Bedford Jail, to groups of simple people in Kilsyth and Lewis and Cambuslang.

What made the Tabernacle worthy of its purpose was not the brass nor the silver not the gold nor the silk, but the thing invisible, intangible, indescribable — the presence of the Glory of the Lord. There was nothing impressive about the first Church — just twelve men in an upper room, unsophisticated, frightened, untried, very unsure of themselves, but there came a sound from heaven and they were filled with the Holy Ghost. And from that handful of the first Christians have come the eleven thousand million who make up the world Church today.

As we face the world in its desperate need, as we reflect on the confusion in our own lives and the disorders of the Church, we may well — we must, despair if we have nothing in which to trust but our own strength or wisdom or goodness. But it is not so. Having done all we can do as well as we can do it, let us realise our own impotence and look to heaven. Let us above all, pray and keep on praying that, as of old, the miracle may again be wrought in the mercy of God, that, once again, the Glory of the Lord may fill the Tabernacle and the Holy Ghost the hearts of those who wait upon Him — that upon us all there may come, as at the beginning, the gift of gifts, without which all our planning, all our endeavours are of no avail, that once again God may pour out His Spirit upon His Church and upon us all.

Remember the handful of ex-slaves, gathered round their goatskin tent in the wilderness, waiting, waiting, until the Glory of the Lord filled the Tabernacle. And remember the handful of simple men in the Upper Room at Jerusalem, gathered with one accord in one place, waiting, waiting till there came a sound from heaven and they were all filled with the Holy Ghost.

It can happen again. It will happen again when we learn to wait upon God.

"The glory of the Lord *filled* the tabernacle."

"They were all *filled* with the Holy Ghost."

TRINITY SUNDAY

Work

John 5.17 (NEB) "My Father has never yet ceased his work, and I am working too."

Romans 8.26 (NEB) "In the same way the Spirit comes to the aid of our weakness."

One of the most helpful ways of thinking of the Three Persons in the Unity of the Godhead is to think of their differing functions. God is one God, but He shows Himself to us, at one time, as God the Father Almighty, Maker of heaven and earth; at another as God the Son, the Saviour of the world; and at another, as God the Spirit, the Renewer of our souls. Fundamentally a unity, they have different functions. They are at one, however, in this, that they all work. "My Father has never yet ceased his work, and I am working too." "The Spirit comes to the aid of our weakness." If it seems to us that there is something improper or vulgar in the thought of God working, it shows that we have the wrong ideas, not only of work, but of God Himself. The God of the Christian revelation is no unmoved mover, no impassive spectator of the world He has made, but a working God — living and active. He is active in creation and preservation, active in redemption, and active, if we but allow Him, in our own hearts and lives.

The Old Testament writers had a very clear idea of the wonderful work of the Creator. "And God saw all that he had made, and it was very good." "When I look up at thy heavens, the work of thy fingers," and, rather quaintly, "It is time to act, O Lord." God scamped nothing in His work of creation, and, whether we consider the starry heavens above, the perfection of detail in a flower, the power in a single atom, or how fearfully and wonderfully we are made, we may say, "Marvellous are thy works."

Christ, when He came, was at one with the Father in the perfection of His work. He was a craftsman on whose bench, we may be sure, no shoddy article was ever made, a manual worker who was not afraid or ashamed to work with His hands. When the time came for His ministry to commence He worked just as hard, ceaselessly preaching, travelling, and healing — healing which cost Him effort and strength. A seven-day week was often His — without time even for meals or sleep. Then came the time when He said to the Father, "I have finished the work which thou gavest me to do." So, He went to fulfill the purpose for which He was born, the causes for which He came into the world. The last work of the Carpenter of Nazareth was to make a bridge from earth to heaven, and He made it in the shape of a Cross. When He knew that all things were accomplished He said, "It is finished," and gave up the ghost. Then came the Resurrection morn with its proof of the all-sufficiency of the work of Christ, and at last His ascension to make intercession for us.

God the Father made the world. God the Son redeemed it. Even yet the work did not finish, and it is not and shall not be finished until every ransomed soul is safely gathered in. This is the work of God the Holy Spirit. The faith that brings us to the Father in penitence, through Christ, is the work of the Holy Spirit. The Spirit teaches us to pray "Abba Father", and empowers us to grow in holiness and grace. He assists us to begin to give the management of our lives to Christ. "My Father has never yet ceased his work, and I am working too." "In the same way the Spirit comes to the aid of our weakness."

What is the application of all this, the point of it for our day? First of all, it is clear that the doctrine of a working God has something to say in the field of politics and social economics. A hundred years ago an industrial burgh in Scotland could take as its motto: "Laborare est orare", "Working is praying". But now, weary of a life of unremitting labour and little leisure, and suspicious of exploitation by

Capitalism, a long campaign has been fought for shorter hours and longer holidays. It is not to deny the need or value of those claims to say that they have had the effect of bringing work into disrepute. Work has become so despised as something to be borne only for the sake of wages, or, at the best, a necessary evil. No longer is it seen as a means of imitating and of serving God. If compulsory unemployment is a crime against God and man, as it is, so also is voluntary idleness and half-hearted labour. There is good sense and good theology in Jack London's parody of a famous hymn:

"Now I get me up to work,
I pray the Lord I may not shirk,
If I should die before the night,
I pray the Lord, my work's all right."

A state which permits or encourages laziness is not only courting disaster but is flouting God, whose will it is that we should serve Him in the service of our fellows in our daily work. "Whatever task lies to your hand, do it with all your might," is sound and scriptural advice.

Nor should we be ashamed of our work, whatever it may be. To say "I'm only a labourer," or "I'm only a housewife," is to be falsely modest. To disparage our work is to disparage God who gave it to us, and who is Himself a worker. Our service of our fellows is service to God, whether we lay gas mains, drive buses, teach, wash dishes, write, sell goods, manage, direct, or even make people laugh and forget their worries. If we do something which is of real use to our fellows, we are of use to God Himself.

If our work is dull or uninteresting, and it seems to help people only a little, we may find in the work of the Church a means of filling up the measure of our service to God and man. Even if we are old and helpless we can work hard at prayer, and find someone to whom we can write or speak a word for Christ. One of the most helpful Christian workers I knew was an old lady of ninety-seven years, whose many visitors never left without hearing some word of testimony to the faith that was in her. Members of the Church are not called to be served by the Church or the ministry, but to be fellow workers with the minister in the work of Christ. It is part of a Christian's duty to seek to gather into the Church, and into the knowledge of God's redeeming love, all of those about him who meantime walk meanly or sadly or blunderingly, for lack of Christ. There is a job for the Church in the world, and there is a job for each and every individual in it. It is our duty to seek and to make and to take, every chance of working for Christ, whose work for us is perfect and complete.

Let us then see to it that God's plan for us, that we should work, is not baulked by bad economics, or by timid, selfish or muddled politics. Let us not be ashamed of our daily work, if it be honest and helpful to our fellows. Let us not be slow or reluctant to work for Christ's Church — to be fellow-labourers with God, servants of Christ, workers with the Holy Spirit. So shall we be caught up into the life of God, and when our day of life is ended, we shall be able to say to God, with Christ, "I have finished the work which thou gavest me to do," and so hear from His lips — "Well done, my good and trusty servant — come and share your master's delight."

—————— · ——————

A Sense of Awe

Acts 2.41-42 (NEB) "Then those who accepted his word were baptized, and some three thousand were added to their number that day. They met constantly to hear the apostles teach, and to share the common life, to break bread, and to pray. A sense of awe was everywhere, and many marvels and signs were brought about through the apostles."

The latest Parish Magazine is available today. I hope it is interesting. But curiously, if it survives 100 years it will be much more interesting. If a copy should survive 500 years it will be a great rarity and if a fragile and yellowing copy should be found somehow in 1900 years, it will cause terrific excitement among scholars, as giving an account of Church life in Scotland in the late twentieth century.

Well, we have a Parish Magazine from the Jerusalem Church of 1900 years ago. It is contained in the second chapter of the Book of Acts. Let me read it to you again: "Then those who accepted his word were baptized, and some three thousand were added to their number that day. They met constantly to hear the apostles teach, and to share the common life, to break bread, and to pray. A sense of awe was everywhere, and many marvels and signs were brought about through the apostles."

As we compare the two Parish magazines, the one from Jerusalem in AD 30 and the other from Dunblane in 1981, there are three striking similarities and three striking differences.

First the similarities. They had baptism — so have we. Our Parish Magazine, like that of Jerusalem, lists several — twelve last month. They broke bread — so do we. Our Magazine tells of the six or seven hundred who broke bread here at our last Communion. They met together to be taught, to have fellowship with each other and to pray. Our Magazine gives details of our services, where there will be teaching and fellowship and prayer.

These are the three similarities which have persisted over nearly two thousand years — baptism, the Lord's Supper and a meeting for teaching, fellowship and prayer.

But there the similarities end. There are three ways in which the contrast between the two Parish magazines is startling — almost painful.

In Jerusalem, about three thousand souls were added in one day. Our Parish Magazine gives a list of precisely nineteen added in the past month.

In Jerusalem, many marvels and signs were brought about through the apostles. Well! Luther once said of his wife, "I suppose I should give thanks for my Anna, for after all she is the gift of God and I suppose there are worse women." I suppose most of you could be persuaded to thank God for your minister, for he is the gift of God, and in all humility, I suppose there are worse ministers. But as for bringing about marvels and signs —! You fortunately don't expect it, for it doesn't happen.

Why is it so? Why does the Church advance so slowly? Why do the ministers do nothing wonderful? Why is the Church so dull, so humdrum, so unexciting? I think the explanation is in the three differences between the Jerusalem Christians and ourselves. It is something that happened before the marvels and wonders were done by the apostles. Listen. "A sense of awe was everywhere." It is this which is lacking, this sense of another dimension, this profound reverence, awe, call it what you will.

It has been said that what we need is an aweful revelation — a revelation full of awe. Obviously the early church had it. The Roman Catholic Church had it, in some sort, with incense and flickering candles and gorgeous robes and what Chesterton called "The holy muttering at the alter" — the sonorous Latin. Most of that is gone and many Roman Catholics miss it terribly. The Reformed Church had it with its stern and terrible preaching and the austere simplicity of the Lord's Supper.

Now we don't have it. Some ministers chat to God as if He were the slightly socially inferior man over the garden wall. To use "Thee" and "Thou" is now almost unknown, but, a poor and imperfect way of expressing our awe of the Lord God Almighty though it was, it was still an attempt. It is true that Jesus said, "When you pray, say 'Our Father'", but immediately, as if to correct any false impression that God is just a good-natured old citizen, He went on "'Which art in Heaven, hallowed' — held in reverence —' be Thy name'."

If there is nothing in the Church that you can't obtain on television or in the theatre or concert hall, then why bother with the Church? But there is. Sometimes at least there is a sense of the Holy, of another dimension, a vertical dimension which cuts clean across our horizontal dimension of work and play, buying and selling, eating and sleeping. Wonder is the basis of religion and the wonder does not diminish with knowing God better. It grows. Kant, the philosopher, said, "Two things fill the mind with ever new and increasing wonder and awe — the starry heavens above me and the moral law within me, and the origin of both is God."

Why do there seem to be no great figures in the Church now, people like Dr John White, Sir George Adam Smith, James Moffat? Is it not just that we know today's leading churchmen? It may be that the nearer we are to great human beings, the less awe-inspiring they seem.

But the nearer one is to God, the more awe-inspiring He becomes. Those who are furthest, walk most humbly with their God. It is the superficial, the Godless, the shallow who can use the name of God lightly. The proof that we are in touch with the Lord God and not with some cheap idol of our own fashioning, will be not the easy familiarity with which we speak of Him or to Him, but the awed and stumbling reticence which baulks our effort to say anything at all about Him.

Today is Trinity Sunday. The doctrine of the Holy Trinity is not a complete description of God but the admission that we cannot describe God completely, that He is Three-in-one and One-in-three, that He is not beyond our knowledge but beyond our comprehension.

If we have really and truly been in touch with God in Christ and felt the brush of His Spirit against our souls, it will show in a certain hushed wonder in our hearts and in our transformed lives. The two are inextricably linked — the knowledge of God and the service of His children. Those who have some awareness of God, who have beheld His glory full of grace and truth in Jesus Christ, and have known the reality of His Spirit in their lives, cannot help but be better men and women. Kinder, truer, braver, more generous will be those whose hearts God has touched.

The knowledge of the Holy Trinity is meant to lead us to holy lives. The twin marks of true religion are awe towards God and great kindness to our fellows. When we who call ourselves Christians show these two qualities, marvels and signs will be done again in the Church and multitudes will be added to the company of Christ.

Before that happens, before the national spiritual renewal which is the precondition of our recovery as a nation can happen, it must happen in you and me. When I allow Christ to work His marvels and signs in me, I can expect to see again, as at the first and as often again since in history, many marvels and signs in the nation and in the world, and great numbers again being added daily to the Church.

What will convince the world — as nothing else will — is the evidence of Christ at work in your life and mine.

CHRISTIAN AID SUNDAY

Life and Food

Matthew 6.25 "Is not life more than food?"

To that the harassed housewife might well answer "not much more". One meal seems hardly to be cleared away before the preparations for the next have to be begun. Hunger, sex and herd are the three basic instincts in our psychological make-up, and of these hunger is probably the strongest. It certainly lasts the longest. It manifests itself with a baby's first cry and continues almost until we draw our last breath. Once I went into a ward of very old people in a hospital. The patients lay absolutely still, not paying the slightest heed to the nurses or to me, completely oblivious to their surroundings or so it seemed. When, however, there was the sound of the food trolley, there was a dramatic change of scene. It was as if the last trump had sounded. Everyone sat bolt upright ready for his meal. From first to last our food is important to us. Let there be the least rumour of a shortage of some commodity — sugar or bread — and we all panic. A friend who was in a prisoner of war camp for officers has told me of seeing cultured, disciplined men fighting over a crust of bread. Only those who have never been near starvation can affect to be superior to the basic, elemental drive of hunger. Dr Johnson, who knew what he was speaking about, once said, "A man seldom thinks with more earnestness than he does of his dinner."

Certainly Jesus knew how important food is. He was bound to know, having been brought up in a widow's home, in a land where famine was not uncommon. His thoughts often turned to bread. In the prayer He taught His disciples, the prayer for bread comes before the prayers for forgiveness and guidance. He defended His disciples for plucking the corn

116

and eating it on the Sabbath Day, when they were hungry. When He sought to find a word to describe himself He said, "I am the bread of life." When He wished to make sure that His disciples would remember him, He gave them a piece of bread and said, "Take, eat. Do this in remembrance of me." There was no doubt in Jesus' mind that whatever else, whatever more, life might be, it is food. We should be equally clear that it is so.

Life is food, but it is more than food. We do not just devour our food like animals. There is more to eating than satisfying a primitive instinct. We have made of every meal something of a sacrament. The wife or mother shows her love by the pains she takes to prepare and serve the food to her family, and they show, or should show, their love by their appreciation of it. Nor is the expression of affection in a meal confined to the members of our immediate family. We are never more distinctly human than when we sit down with friends, in their home or ours, to a well-planned, well-cooked, well-served meal.

This is true not only of Christian people, but of those of any religion or of none. Those who call Christ Lord, however, differ from others in that they cannot restrict their hospitality to their friends and relatives on a strictly "chop for chop" basis. Jesus once said, "If you only love those who love you, what credit is that to you? Even sinners love those who love them." Our claim to a share in the love of Christ depends on the fact that He has placed no sort of restriction upon it. Since this is so we cannot shut our ears to the cries nor our hearts to the need of those for whom also Christ was content to die. The only way in which we can show our gratitude to Christ for what He has done for us is by what we do for others. This is the only way in which we can even begin to pay our immeasurable debt.

When the Son of Man shall come in His glory, this is how we shall be judged: "Then the king will say to those on his right hand, 'You have my Father's blessing; come, enter and possess the kingdom that has been ready for you since the world was made. For when I was hungry, you gave me food — I tell you this: anything you did for one of my brothers here, however humble, you did it for me'."

We cannot, therefore, dare not, be indifferent to the fact that hundreds of millions of those whom Christ has called His brothers are at this very moment literally starving in Africa and India, in South America and South East Asia. Jesus, we read, had compassion when He saw the multitude because they had nothing to eat. He refused to send them away fasting and ready to faint. If we have anything of His spirit, a like compassion will move us to help.

Life is food for ourselves and it is food shared with others, with those whose only claim upon us is their hunger and the fact that they are our brothers and sisters in Christ. But life is more even than shared food. There is that in man which cannot be satisfied with even the richest and most ample diet. There is that within all of us which cannot be content with mere things. We are all at times conscious of:

"The restless throbbings and burnings
That Hope unsatisfied brings,
The weary longings and yearnings
For mystical better things."

We try to satisfy our secret, deep desires with more and more of this world's goods, more pleasure, more comfort, longer holidays, more and more expensive food and drink. We seek to suppress our disgust and secret loathing for the things we claim to enjoy. We attempt to hide the deep weariness and sated lust which make of human life a hell. But it will not do. Life *is* more than food, however hard we may try to make ourselves believe otherwise. The "more" in which life consists is nothing less, nothing other than God. "Give us of Thyself," cried Augustine, "without which cannot we be satisfied though thou shouldest give us all else that ever thou hast made." Life is food, but if we look at it with honest eyes in all its majesty and mystery, we know that it is more than food, much more.

In sorrow once Christ said "I know you have not come looking for me because you saw signs, but because you ate the bread and your hunger was satisfied. You must work, not for this perishable food, but for the food that lasts, the food of eternal life. This food the Son of Man will give you." And again, "I am the bread of life. Whoever comes to me shall never be hungry." That must be said and said with force and emphasis to those who are trying, in our materialistic society, to satisfy their souls' hunger with their bodies' bread. But it cannot be said to those whose bodies are starving.

The more clearly we have heard Christ's command to go into all the world and preach the Gospel to every creature, and the more eager we are to obey it, the more we shall find ourselves forced to try first to satisfy the hunger of mens' bodies. Christian Aid is not an optional extra for the Christian mission in the world. It is a necessary concommitant — perhaps even a necessary preliminary to it. Only as their basic hunger for bread is satisfied will men be able to look beyond the clamant needs of their bodies, and to find life in its fulness not in eating and drinking but in Jesus Christ, who first asked: "Is not life more than food?"

HARVEST THANKSGIVING

Food in Due Season

Psalm 145.15-16 (RSV) "The eyes of all look to thee, and thou givest them their food in due season. Thou openest thy hand, thou satisfiest the desire of every living thing."

That sounds fine but is it true? I would suggest:

1. That it is true for us only if we are prepared to co-operate by our own hard work.

2. That it is true for us only if we are prepared to co-operate by sharing the wealth we enjoy.

3. That it is true in the deepest sense only if we are prepared to do what God commands and to receive what God is eager to give — Himself in Christ who is the bread of life.

1. It is true that God gives us our food and satisfies our desires only if we are prepared to co-operate by our own hard work.

It is so easy to talk about fields of golden grain, of the orchards with their bountiful crops, the joyous harvesters, the luscious fruits, the abundant providing of God. It is easy and it is right that we should once a year acknowledge with gratitude the food we enjoy in such variety and abundance, and the flowers God has given to delight our hearts. But before God gives us food to satisfy our desire, there's a lot of work to be done by us. Ask any farmer or gardener or fisher or miner what would happen if he sat by the fire and waited for God to shower grain or fish or fruit or coal on his head.

Before going on to speak of lush crops and bountiful harvests and mellow fruitfulness, we need to hear the astringent message of Genesis. "Cursed is the ground — in toil you shall eat of it all the days of your life; thorns and thistles it shall bring forth to you — in the sweat of your face you shall eat

120

bread till you return to the earth." How true that is. Sweat before sweetness.

I remember one year asking a farming friend why a great many of my potatoes were black at the heart. He told me it was due to wet weather early on. "And why," I asked him "have my carrots split?" "Ah, that is due to dry weather later on." It sometimes seems you can't win. There is a certain thrawnness in the soil. This year we've had leaf curl, black spot, mildew and red spider on the Manse roses. It's a marvel any have survived. It is obvious that God has no intention of allowing us to lie back and take it easy and have our every desire satisfied without effort or thought on our part.

And that is a lesson we need to learn anew, especially here in Britain, where we have been eating the seed-corn too long. The world does not owe us a living — nor does God. Unemployment is a great curse, but it will not be removed until we all learn to demand less from the common pool and to work harder for what we get. Whether we are labourers or students or farmers or ministers, we should be ashamed to eat our bread and take our rest unless we have put in a decent day's work and unless we are ready to share the fruit of our work with any who cannot work or cannot find work.

St Paul was quite clear on the point "If anyone will not work, let him not eat." With quietness we should work and eat our own bread. God will give us food only if we are prepared to play our part.

2. He will give others their food only if we are prepared to share. No man lives unto himself. To survive at all, we are dependant on the exertions of many besides ourselves. None of us could make a living from three acres and a cow nowadays.

Think even of what you had for breakfast — milk and cereal, porridge if you want to avoid heart disease, tea with sugar, bread and marmalade perhaps? For that we have to thank the farmer for the dairy produce, the delivery man for bringing the milk, the maker of his van with its thousands of component parts, Canadians possibly for the cereal and wheat for the bread. The ship which brought them across the Atlantic was built by hundreds of artisans and manned by dozens of sailors. The tea came probably from India, involving the labours of pickers and blenders, the sugar from Jamaica and the marmalade oranges from Spain and so on. We are all involved in a vast network of supply and demand in which we are all dependant on everybody else.

I was talking this week with a lady weighed down with the shopping she had just done for her household of four. God has to feed four thousand million every day. The wonder is not that the system sometimes breaks down with over-production and unemployment and the like, but that it works at all. We depend — each of us — on ourselves, on our own labour and initiative, on our own energy and faithfulness; we depend on others, on the honesty and skill of a vast complex of people who make up the world community; and

3. they depend on us — and many, many millions of them depend in vain. Our co-operation is needed, not only for God to supply our own needs but equally for God to supply the needs of others.

"The eyes of all look to thee, and thou givest them their food in due season. Thou openest thy hand, thou satisfiest the desire of every living thing."

It's not true. It's just not true. In India, in South and Central America, in Ethiopia, the eyes of millions of men, women and children hungrily and hopelessly scan the heavens and scan the heavens in vain because of our failure to solve the problem of feeding the world's hungry. We expend our ingenuity on video-recorders and word processors, on expeditions to the planets. We spend our money on tanks rather than on tractors, on gunboats instead of fishing boats.

Have we the right to thank God for His plentiful provision for us? Have we the right to enjoy the fruits of our harvest unless we are prepared to make much more strenuous efforts to share His bounty with all our brothers and sisters throughout the world, to be God's instruments in His longing to satisfy the desires of every living thing, and not for their sakes alone but for our own? For, until we do so, until we are really ashamed that even one of our four thousand million brothers and sisters is hungry for bread, God cannot satisfy our own desperate hunger of soul. Our deepest, most lasting hunger is not for food nor for any of the delights of life. Our deepest hunger is for God.

"Give me of thyself", said Augustine, "without which, though thou shouldest give me all else that thou hast made, yet could I not be satisfied." If we can honestly echo that prayer and find it to be answered in Him who said, "I am the bread of life; he who comes to me shall not hunger", we should not find it hard to give ourselves in love to others. It is only as we do that we can receive in all its fullness the gift that beggars all God's other gifts, the gift of Himself to be our Saviour.

When we receive this gift, we shall see our harvest gifts as the merest token of a service to Christ and to our fellows that would set no limits, and of a giving that would hold nothing back from Him who held nothing back from us. Those who have received Christ's love and have responded in love to Him and to the least of His brethren, can say with a fullness of meaning the Psalmist never knew:

"The eyes of all look to thee, and thou givest them their food in due season. Thou openest thy hand, thou satisfiest the desire of every living thing."

Jesus said, "I am the bread of life; he who comes to me shall not hunger, and he who believes in me shall never thirst."

ALL SAINTS DAY

Saints at Philippi

Philippians 1.1 "Paul and Timotheus, the servants of Jesus Christ, to all the saints in Christ Jesus which are at Philippi."

New Testament cities sound such beautifully holy places, but they were nothing of the kind. Jerusalem, Nazareth, Bethlehem were no different, no better than any other Middle Eastern cities. And Philippi, although Paul seems to have had a special affection for the church there, was nothing very wonderful. Certainly it was not the secluded sort of spot conducive to a cloistered piety. It was a garrison town with the usual quota of vice and crime typical of such places, and with busy shops and crowded streets.

What of those who made up the church there? Were they a specially selected group of "religious", keeping themselves unspotted from the pagan environment in which they lived? It would not seem so. Lydia was one of the members, and she was a prominent business woman. Another member was the governor of the prison and a third an epileptic slave girl. These were ordinary people going about their ordinary business in a then modern town — just such a group as could be found in an average congregation in any big town today. "Ah yes," you say, "but surely these people whom Paul called saints were different from the average church member of today." Although they may have followed their ordinary callings in a bustling pagan city, they must have had an eagerness for their new-found faith, an eagerness which has faded with the passing centuries, a holiness which has grown stale. They must have been different from today's church members if Paul could call them, as a group, "the saints at Philippi".

Were they so very different? We read in the New Testament

of quite disgraceful behaviour among the members of the early Church, of open quarrels and silly heresies, of men struggling for power, of folk growing weary of the Gospel and falling away. In this very letter Paul says, "Beware of dogs, beware of evil workers". The occasion of the letter was a fight between women members of the congregation, which had caused a great scandal. These were the people whom Paul called "the saints at Philippi". Was he being sarcastic? If not, what did he mean?

Partly it is, of course, that we need to define our terms, to be more clear what we mean by "saint". In the Reformed Church we have never quite made up our minds on the subject. We have rather unthinkingly taken over the mediaeval usage by which "saint" is spelled with a capital "S", and restricted it in use to those, long dead, who were believed to have been exceptionally good. We use it in this way for the first disciples and for most of those called "Saint" by the mediaeval Church — people like Augustine, Columba, Bernard, and Francis. Rather strangely, however, we have assumed that no "Saint" in that sense has appeared since the sixteenth century. Perhaps a case could be made out for, say, Saint Mary Slessor, or Saint Albert Schweitzer. But who are we to assess degrees of holiness? We would be far better to abandon the use of "Saint" with a capital "S" altogether, in favour of the New Testament usage. There it is applied to all who have been called of God. The really significant phrase in the text is "in Christ Jesus".

It was not to a particularly holy city that Paul wrote, nor to a holy enclave in a predominantly heathen city, but to ordinary men and women, some better, some worse; some wise, some foolish; some more faithful, some less so. All that at first distinguished them from their pagan neighbours was that they were "in Christ Jesus". As time passed, being in Christ led them to grow in love for each other and in purity of life. Finally they grew into the very likeness of Christ Himself — but not at first. Certainly they were not inherently superior to their heathen neighbours, and there was nothing different about them in the end except what their calling in Christ could explain. Brodie of Brodie once said of himself, "I am a reeling, unstable, staggering, unsettled, lukewarm creature, but my Lord can carve a saint out of worse timber, if worse there be, and *all rests finally* with Him." That is the nub of the matter. "All rests finally with Christ." The saints are simply the friends of Christ, those of no distinction of themselves whom He has chosen to be of His company, "For all the saints who from their labours rest", we sing. It is right to salute the saints in heaven, for they were great souls, and some of them were dear to our own hearts. But all of them before they were saints in heaven were saints on earth, striving to live the Christian life in some Philippi not of their choosing.

You and I may aspire to be among their number, but not by trying to be better than others. That way lies hypocrisy. The way towards sanctity is by yielding ourselves more fully to Christ. The world stands in danger of self-destruction, the nation is beset with problems that seem insoluble, and the Church is ineffective and sterile, not for lack of great and noble heroes of the faith, nor for lack of perfect Christians, but for lack of ordinary people who have yielded themselves into the hands of Christ to be used for His purposes. You and I may seem to ourselves to be instruments curiously unfit for the Master's use — ungainly, liable to come apart, if the least pressure be put upon us. But it's not our strength that matters, not our wisdom or goodness, but His. All He requires is a little humility and a willingness to be used. If we have that, we need have no fear of being excluded from Christ's service any more than those whose address Paul wrote, with such confidence that it would reach them, "To all the saints in Christ Jesus which are at Philippi".

With All the Saints

Ephesians 3.17-19 "That you, being rooted and grounded in love, may have power to comprehend with all the saints what is the breadth and length and height and depth, and to know the love of Christ which surpasses knowledge."

"To comprehend with all the saints."

Today is kept by some churches as All Saints Day, tomorrow as All Souls Day. We don't pay much attention to that kind of thing in Scotland. We don't pray to the dead nor for them and rightly so, for the dead are in the hands of God, they do not need our prayers. But I wonder if we are right to ignore them as we so often try to do — the month's mind and the year's mind were old Scottish customs and it is a pity they have fallen into disuse.

There is only a comparative handful of us alive in the world at this moment. Most people are among those whom men call dead. If we believe in democracy, should we not give some weight to their opinions? On any counting of heads they are in the majority, and they have contributed far more to our country and our world than we have done. Think what we owe to those gone before us. The inventions — printing and television, electricity and penicillin, the telephone and the aeroplane and so much else. We stand on the shoulders of the great thinkers and writers and artists and composers and poets — Burns, Beethoven, Rembrandt and Shakespeare. We stand on their shoulders and see further because of them. We should not forget the debt we owe. We stand on the shoulders of countless others too, obscure folk who built roads and bridges, ploughed fields, planted forests, made laws, fought for freedom and passed on to us the Faith. They have laboured and we have entered into their labours. We should be thankful for the dead.

"For there's another country I've heard of long ago
Most dear to them that love her, most great to them that know.
We may not count her armies, we may not see her king
Her fortress is a faithful heart, her pride is suffering.
And soul by soul and silently her shining bounds increase
Her ways are ways of gentleness and all her paths are peace."

Of course our duty is to the living and we must forever be applying the Gospel to the pressing problems that confront us in the real world of today, but that we shall do only as we bring to bear upon the problems of the passing world the perspective of eternity. As soon as the world forgets eternity, it becomes gross and quarrelsome and stupid. That is why we need to be reminded, when we become despondent and uncertain, that we are fellow citizens with the saints of the household of God.

An embassy in a foreign country may be an inconspicuous enough building, but it represents a great nation. We who are of the Church in the world are ambassadors for Christ and should have a proper pride in the fact that however few we may be, we represent the countless throng of the redeemed who have been made kings and priests to God.

However split up the denominations, the True Church is one and undivided. St John and St Paul, St Augustine and Martin Luther, Livingstone and Mary Slessor, Albert Schweitzer and Eric Liddell and those still in the world known to us and unknown, who love Christ a little and would fain know and love and serve Him better, — and those yet to be.

"One family we dwell in Him,
One Church above, beneath."

The Church as we know it in our day is only a snapshot of the majestic procession of the saints from their origin in God to their place in the Church Triumphant in heaven.

Think of the people who have worshipped in this church through the ages — bishops and priests, noblemen and shepherds, tradesmen and soldiers, saints and sinners.

Tens of thousands, hundreds of thousands of men and women of like passion with ourselves, whose blood still flows in our veins, though we cannot see them, worship with us still, for we share with them One Lord, One Faith, One Baptism.

We worship today with all the saints. We view the world today with all the saints. We lay hold upon the life of Christ with all the saints. A majestic thought, but does it really help us to know that we are "compassed about with so great a cloud of witnesses"? Will it help us to keep our sanity in a world gone mad? I think it will.

Here is cheer for the evil day. How much more were the saints called to endure than we — the lions in the arena, the rack, the thumbscrew, torture and flames. But they fought a good fight. They kept the faith and so they have received the crown of righteousness. If we can but lay hold of that, lay hold of the assurance of their victory that

". . . when the strife is fierce, the warfare long,

Steals on the ear the distant triumph song,

And hearts are brave again, and arms are strong."

The saints must get many a smile as we panic about the state of the world and of the nation, and gloomily await the speedy end of the Church. They ask us "Why so despondent and afraid? God also is wise. He has His plans which span eternity. Keep your sense of humour which is just a sense of proportion. See the happenings of your little day against the background of His mighty purpose. We have lived in the world too," they say, "and fought and worried, and now through Christ have won the victory."

Yet of course the saints were victorious only because they greatly cared and greatly dared. So, as well as cheer for the evil day, the communion of saints is an encouragement and strength for the duties that lie before us.

It is because they did not fail that we have received the heritage of the Faith. So we too must fling our handful of seed to the wind. We too must lay our pebble on the cairn. We too must strike our blow in the everlasting battle of right with wrong, of good with evil, of love with hate. There is no need to panic but there is need to care. There is no cause for desperation but there is cause for concern. Christ will not fail us but we must not fail Him.

So let us see ourselves as soldiers in the mighty army of the Church of God, bound together by the strategy of Christ, each of us with a little part to play, each of us with a limited version of the Master Plan of God, each of us with a place prepared for us in the Father's house with all the saints. We're in good company now and we shall be in better.

Of course there is much that is obscure, that we do not and cannot understand. But so it was with all the saints. Often weary, often perplexed they kept the Faith and so shall we, if we, like them, keep close to Christ. This is the link that binds us to them.

> "Death doth hide but not divide
> Thou art but on Christ's other side.
> Christ with thee and Christ with me
> With Him together still are we."

And so we shall, and then in a way that is not now possible, we shall be able to comprehend "what is the breadth and length and height and depth, and to know the love of Christ which surpasses knowledge" — "with all the saints".

REMEMBRANCE DAY

Introduction

Shortly we shall be quiet for two minutes, which is not much time to give for those who gave their whole lives. How shall we fill that time?

For some, two minutes will be too short. Their thoughts will be of someone they could never forget, someone whom they lost. For some of us, those who died were our contemporaries and our friends. We remember their courage, their gaiety and their kindness, and always will.

But most of you are too young to remember. How can you fill in those two minutes? You can pray for those who are sad today, and for those who were blinded or made into invalids by war's cruelty.

All of us will pray for those still in danger in Ulster and elsewhere; for children in many lands homeless and hungry because of war. And all of us will pray for peace, and will dedicate ourselves anew to working for the justice for all the members of God's family from which alone true peace will come. Then we shall listen for God to speak.

———————— · ————————

A Book of Remembrance was Written

Malachi 3.16 "Then they that feared the Lord spake often one to another: and the Lord hearkened, and heard it, and a book of remembrance was written before him."

When times were bad in Israel, when religion and morals decayed, when corruption was rife, when on every hand there was fear and suspicion and despair, the Israelites did a wise thing. They looked back, to find in their great past inspiration to face the unknown future.

First of all they remembered their great and good men with whose names their history was studded — Noah and Abraham, Isaac and Jacob, Joseph and Moses, Gideon, Barak, Samson and Jephthae, David and Samuel and a host of other unnamed heroes and saints. Then they recalled the great events of their history — how they had come out of exile in Egypt and had conquered Palestine, how they had battled with the super-powers Egypt and Syria and had never quite been defeated, how they had survived even the second long exile in Babylon. Having remembered their great men and the great events of their history, they remembered how it had all been accomplished by the mercy and guidance of their great God.

The times in which Malachi lived were evil times. The priesthood had become corrupt; the pure religion of the Jews had been debased by being mixed with the heathenism round about; there was widespread poverty — some parents were even selling their children as slaves — divorce was rife, men repudiating the wives of their youth when they no longer pleased them; sorcery — black magic — was common. People were beginning to doubt if there was any sense or reality in religion.

But a few good men remained. They talked to each other and thought back to all the way they had been led. "Then the Lord hearkened and heard it, and a book of remembrance was written before him."

The Persian kings had a custom of keeping a book of remembrance in which was written the name of anyone who had served the State well, so that in due course he might receive a suitable reward. This is the picture which Malachi has here — of a great book of remembrance in which all the names of heroes and humble faithful souls should be written.

There is much in our own country and throughout the world

at this moment which is bad — unemployment, inflation, soaring rates of crime and alcoholism, sexual laxity, hooliganism and vandalism of every sort. Sometimes it seems there is no honour, no sense of duty, no discipline, no real religion left.

If, thinking of all this, we are tempted to lose heart, we should think of our great past and of the great figures of our history — sailors like Drake and Nelson, soldiers like Wellington and Montgomery, reformers like Shaftesbury and Elizabeth Fry, missionaries like Livingstone and Mary Slessor, politicians like Disraeli, Gladstone and Churchill, poets like Shakespeare, Milton and Burns. And we should remember the great events of our history — how we stood three times against the might of Europe under Napoleon, the Kaiser and Hitler. The fashion now is to decry the British Empire, but there has never been an empire with a better record of honest government and enlightened service of subject peoples. It is our language, our traditions of parliamentary democracy which have prevailed in most of our former territories. There is much of which we can be proud, and much for which we should be grateful, as we look back on our long history.

On this day we look back on two world wars and other costly conflicts. We remember with gratitude deliverances like Dunkirk, the Battle of Britain and the Battle of the Atlantic, and remember with pride the men and women of the services and the civilians who put duty first, who did not turn aside from sacrifice, who served faithfully and who died serving.

With our times so out of joint, with so much to make us despair, let us proudly and lovingly take up and handle again our book of remembrance before the Lord. All is *not* sordid calculation and dissipated selfishness, all is *not* cruelty and brutality in a world which held such men and women as those we remember. So our book of remembrance should be kept, and should be read for its honoured names and for its great events.

But if our remembrance today is of men and events, of battles and wars *only*, we might be better to forget, lest we be led to the pride and vengefulness which breed war. If our remembrance is of God, we cannot help but recall that He who revealed God to us asked to be remembered not by victory but by defeat, by broken bread and wine poured out, and by a cross. It is as we seek to imitate that sacrifice that we shall be closest in spirit to those who have died in war, and will do as much as lies in us to ensure that their sacrifice shall not have been in vain.

The community in its need lies about us. The young people in their perplexities look to us, the nations of the world cry out to us in their hunger and fear. It is as we dedicate ourselves afresh to meet those needs that we shall best remember those who sacrificed their lives and shall most faithfully serve Him who died that we, and they, might live.

"Then they that feared the Lord spake often one to another, and the Lord hearkened, and heard it, and a book of remembrance was written before him."

War's Moral Equivalent

Micah 4.3 (NEB) "They shall beat their swords into mattocks and their spears into pruning-knives; nation shall not lift sword against nation, nor ever again be trained for war."

It is 2500 years since Micah spoke these words, and during all these years the prayers for peace have not ceased nor the longing for it disappeared. Nor in all that time has there been a period when there was peace over all the earth. Since Micah wrote, tens, hundreds, thousands, millions have been slaughtered in war, countless hearts have broken and still the cry goes up "How long, O Lord, how long?" No other desire so ancient, so deep, so fervent as the desire for peace has gone so long unsatisfied.

Of course, war is not the only evil. There's hunger and disease, poverty and ignorance. But how much could be done to alleviate these but for the crippling cost of war past, present and to come — thousands of millions spent each year on armaments. Think of weary peasants with wooden ploughs yoked to oxen, dying for the tractors and irrigation pumps which could be made by the same firms which now manufacture arms. The world's need for ploughs and pruning-knives is as great as in Micah's day. The world's swords and spears cost so much more, and can cause so much more pain and death. War — modern war — is evil and wasteful beyond all things: wasteful of armaments if they are not used, and even more wasteful if they are used. All of us are pacifists in the sense that we all want peace. All of us are in favour of disarmament if we have any sense in us — far less any religion. We may differ as to the best means of achieving peace and disarmament, but we can unite in seeing peace as our greatest priority for our nation and the nations of the world. If we achieve peace all future generations will call us blessed. If we fail there will be no future generations to call us accursed. The causes of war must be isolated and eliminated if the world is to survive.

There are no words we can find sufficiently to express our detestation of war: yet paradoxically, out of war come some things that are good. The marvellous sense of comradeship in the services, the knowledge that each depends on all and all on each, the feeling of belonging to each other. Joined in a great cause, courage and nobility come to light in the most ordinary human beings.

Not many of you here knew men who died, but I knew them well. Next door to my cabin at Scapa Flow was a Glasgow business man turned mine disposal officer. When gales brought mines ashore or close to ships, he would be called out, often in the middle of the night. He would always look in to see me before he left on one of these missions, and he always looked in when he came back. One night I waited and waited and he did not come back. He was grave and cheerful. He knew the risks he was taking and undertook them for the sake of others. We should delight to honour the memory of such men and women and to keep alive the spirit that fills them.

If only we could have the good by-products of war — the self-sacrifice, the courage, the comradeship, the social advance — without the war to breed them. This is the fundamental problem we face — to find a moral equivalent of war, to find something which will evoke gallantry and self-sacrifice and encourage true comradeship which is not geared to the destruction of others.

Micah was a Jew and like all his race, economical. He did not want the spear and the sword to be thrown away or destroyed. He wanted them to be reshaped for the purposes of peace. "They shall beat their swords into mattocks and their spears into pruning-knives." We must not despise the idealism, the discipline, the self-sacrifice of those who died, but rather try to draw forth these very same qualities for purposes of good, for the service of God and man.

Hubert Simpson tells of a South Sea island where the drums once used to summon to a cannibal feast are now used as a church bell, and the stone on which human sacrifices were once cut up is used as a baptismal font. Is this unseemly? Surely not. For this is what God does. He takes that which has been used for evil and uses it for good, for the evil is not in the thing itself but in the heart of the man or woman who wields it. The atomic energy which can destroy men can enrich their lives. The bacteriological research which can lead to the most horrible type of war can be used to heal man's diseases. This is the problem of the fight against nuclear and chemical weapons and the like. The evil is not in the weapons themselves but in those who would wield them.

This is at once the hopefulness and the difficulty of the quest for peace. The quest is hopeful, for human nature *can* be changed, but difficult, for nothing can change human nature short of the mighty act of God in Jesus Christ. Christ Jesus came to save sinners. That does not mean only so that we may go to heaven when we die, but so that we may be saved from sinning and so learn to do His work in the world He loved.

As He looks at our fear-racked world, surely the chief desire of the Prince of Peace is that we should give ourselves far more eagerly than we have done to bring this ancient prophecy to pass, "They shall beat their swords into mattocks and their spears into pruning-knives" so that "nation shall not lift sword against nation, nor ever again be trained for war." The only one who can teach us so to do is He who conquered by suffering, who took the ugly, barbarous instrument of His own sore death and out of it forged the means of a world's redemption. By His cross, Christ shows us, if we will but learn, how to turn swords into mattocks and spears into pruning-knives.

Here is the moral equivalent of war — the service of Christ, the only service big enough to match man's hidden greatness and wasting gallantry. The service of Christ can call out all that we have and are, the utmost in devotion and sacrifice. Here is an aim that is bigger than life, a purpose that is greater than self, the service which alone gives perfect freedom.

ST ANDREW'S TIDE

Hadad

1 Kings 11.21 (NEB) "Hadad . . . said to Pharaoh, 'Let me go so that I may return to my own country.' 'What is it that you find wanting in my country?' said Pharaoh. . . 'Nothing,' said Hadad, 'but do, pray, let me go'."

According to Dr Johnson, "Patriotism is the last refuge of the scoundrel." There is enough truth in that to deliver us from using St Andrew's Day as an excuse for an outburst of rabid nationalism or even for municipal or academic chauvinism! St Andrew himself was distinguished among the disciples as being the only one of whom it is recorded that he brought foreigners to Jesus. Through the centuries, it is perhaps a tribute to his internationalism that he has been claimed as Patron Saint not only by Scotland, but by countries as different as Greece and Russia. We in Scotland have not, at our best, been narrowly nationalistic. To quote Johnson again, there is some truth in his assertion that "the fairest prospect for a Scotsman is the high road to England" — en route for the high seas or for far distant lands. For every St Andrews Society in Scotland, there must be a hundred in other parts of the world — in the USA, Australia, New Zealand — even in England.

Apart probably for the Jews, no race has shown a greater capacity than our own for making themselves at home in other lands and achieving some measure of success and distinction. Two Prime Ministers this century, Bonar Law and Campbell Bannerman, were educated at Glasgow High School. Balfour, McDonald, McMillan and Douglas Home bring the total of Scots to occupy 10 Downing Street this century to six. Napoleon's great general was McDonald, Grieg was the founder of the Russian Navy and Keith of Prussian might.

Almost all the great commercial houses of the East have Scottish names — McKinnon McKenzie, Jardine Mathieson, John Stewart and Co., Finlays, Cargills, Dalgetys — all founded and carried on by men exiled from their native land.

Such was Hadad. While still a lad, he was taken by some of his father's servants as a refugee to Egypt. There he was received with kindness. He must have been an attractive lad, for he became a great favourite with Pharaoh. When he grew to man's estate he was given a wife, the Queen's sister. So the links that tied Hadad to the land of his adoption grew stronger. Bye and bye his first son was born and given the Egyptian name Genubah. Queen Tahpenes took a great interest in her nephew and had Genubah brought up in the royal nursery. Hadad, who had come to Egypt as a penniless refugee, had "arrived". Brother-in-law to the Pharaoh, his boy brought up along with his cousin, the future Pharaoh, he had done well for himself, had Hadad. He had all that the heart of man could desire. He was content.

One day there came the news that his father's old enemy was dead and suddenly all was changed. Hadad knew that he must go home. He said to Pharaoh, "Let me go, so that I may return to my own country." Pharaoh could hardly believe his ears, so long had Hadad been at court, that his foreign origin had almost been forgotten. He had seemed perfectly settled. Then suddenly came this odd request. The Queen would be horrified. How could Hadad think of taking *her* sister and nephew — used to all the comforts of the city — to the barbarous hill country of Edom. The King wonders if Hadad has some grievance, some unsatisfied ambition. "What is it that you find wanting in my country, that you want to go back to your own?" Hadad does not try to explain the longing that has seized him. He knows that he can't. It is not a rational thing. It is beyond words and so he answers, "Nothing, but do pray, let me go." Hadad has no complaint about the country of his adoption. He lacks nothing — nothing but the feel of his own country under his feet, the music of his mother-tongue in his ears, the scenery of his own land to gaze at and the knowledge of his own kith and kin about him. He lacks nothing but these, but lacking these he lacks everything.

Robert Louis Stevenson knew the pangs.

> "Be it granted me to behold again in dying
> Hills of home, and to hear again the call
> Hear above the graves of the martyrs the peewees crying
> And hear no more at all."

So it has ever been. God has set in the hearts of every normal human being a love of his or her native land. We belong to the land in which we were born and nowhere else can we be so at home. Of course if we cannot make a living or find a home or if duty demands, we must go elsewhere. All over the world there are the graves of Scots people, forced by poverty or persecution or driven by duty or missionary zeal, to live and die in a strange land. There is always a pathos about emigrants, for after a time they know that they cannot return to their native land, nor yet be entirely happy in the land of their adoption. There is this longing for home in the hearts of us all.

Yet despite this, there is a steady stream of emigrants from this country and a constant stream of people from distant lands wishing to settle here. One wonders if both movements have not, perhaps, a common origin. Do not both — the restlessness of the emigrant and the homesickness of the exile — perhaps come from man's deep, ineradicable, often unrecognised need of God? Is not this same deep need behind the restlessness, the discontents of our time?

> "The restless throbbings and burnings
> That hope unsatisfied brings,
> The weary longings and yearnings
> For the mystical better things."

Hadad's longing may not have been so much for his country as for his country's God. Not all the glory and riches of Egypt could meet the need. Our lives are rich and comfortable, yet it is not enough. Sometimes there comes news from a far country and a strange disquiet comes within us, and an urgent longing which nothing here can satisfy. As Thomas Carlyle once said, "The misfortune of man has its source in his greatness, for there is something infinite in him and he cannot succeed in burying himself completely in the finite." And that is true. There is something in all of us that hungers for that better than the best which the world provides.

The God who made the human heart knew that there are longings deep down within it which none but He can satisfy. When the longing for our hearts' true home in Him is like to turn to despair, He comes in Christ to lead us safely to Himself.

"Thou hast made us for Thyself," cried Augustine, "and our hearts are restless till they find their rest in Thee."

As we look at the joys God has given us in this world — beauty and laughter, work and play, friendship and love — we may say, with Hadad, that we lack nothing. But if we search our hearts, we shall discover a longing that the world cannot satisfy, a need the world cannot meet.

It is a good world this. Let's not despise it. But, at its very best, it is not enough.

"Hadad . . . said to Pharaoh, 'Let me go so that I may return to my own country.' 'What is it that you find wanting in my country?' said Pharaoh. . . 'Nothing,' said Hadad, 'but do, pray, let me go'."

CONFIRMATION

Made Any Good Vows Lately?

Isaiah 19.21 (RSV) "They will make vows to the Lord and perform them."

Made any good vows lately? Of course you haven't. We don't go in much for vows these days and we sit pretty lightly to those we do make. We prefer to play life by ear, to wander through it as the notion takes us, following each byway we come to. Vows we associate with mediaeval superstition — with hair shirts and long pilgrimages and abstention from meat. They seem foreign and unnatural to our more casual view.

Yet all those who have made any significant contribution to the life of the world built their lives on vows — Jacob, Samson, David and Saul in the Old Testament and Paul in the New. Abraham Lincoln's life-long struggle against slavery stemmed from a vow he made when he saw a woman sold like a beast in the market place. Albert Schweitzer's dedication to Africa arose from a vow he made in front of the statue of a black woman. The Reformation which delivered us from so much spiritual tyranny and superstition began with Martin Luther. In his biography of Luther, Bainton calls the first chapter "The Vow", and traces the Reformation to the vow Luther made under stress of great fear.

In our daily lives we are dependent on other people keeping vows they have made. When the Queen came to the throne, she made a vow of service, and right faithfully and nobly she has kept it. The law depends on the utter impartiality of the judges in their honouring the oaths of office they are required to make. So too as regards the police. One in ten thousand may themselves break the law, but generally we may trust

142

them completely. Each time you visit a doctor you are consulting someone under a solemn vow — "I shall act for the benefit of my patients and not for any wrong. I shall give no deadly drug. Whatsoever house I enter, there will I go for the benefit of the sick. Whatsoever I see or hear, I will keep silence thereon, counting such things as sacred secrets."

So too in our personal lives, the stability of the home, the glory of marriage depend on vows seriously made and honourably kept. "Do you take this woman to be your wedded wife and do you promise and covenant in the presence of God and before this congregation to be to her a loving, faithful and dutiful husband until God shall separate you for a time by death?"

On these vows the whole fabric of society depends. They give dignity and nobility to human life and distinguish it from the unreasoning life of the animals. In a world where there is so much drifting, so much dreary, aimless living, let us make our vows and keep them.

So, surely, in the most important matters of all — with regard to religion. We should not leave the matter of our final destiny to the whim of the moment, nor allow our relationship to God to be determined by what we happen to feel like at the time. Human nature is very weak and needs to be undergirded by solemn promises made when our vision is clear. Such vows will be made by the first communicants at this service, but it will be well for us if every one of us renews the vows that we made in time past — some of us a long time ago.

In the wide mouth of the St Lawrence River, no land is visible, but bell buoys mark out the channel in what seems a trackless waste but is really the entrance to the life of a great country. So, too, in a life without landmarks or headlands, we can help ourselves and our fellows by taking up a definite position, saying, "This, this and this I will do and that, that, and that I will not do — so help me God."

That, of course, is the secret. "They will make vows to the

Lord." It is easy enough to make great resolves and even easier to break them, unless we make them to God. The beginning of any sort of nobility in life is the encounter with God. Without Him, the world, the flesh and the devil will prove too much for us. The more we reproach ourselves for failing to keep our vows the more likely we are to break them again. But any real experience of God in His holiness and love, will move us to make vows and help us to keep them.

The word "sacrament" means an oath of allegiance. Part of the meaning of the Lord's Supper, in which we shall join soon, is a public renewal of our allegiance. Who can come near to God without deciding that there can be, must be, will be a change? Face to face with God you can't just say "Good day" and then "Excuse me" and pass on. There must be some clear and precise and definite response. "They will make vows to the Lord — and perform them." That's the secret without which any religious experience can be a wild rush of blood to the head.

So let our vow not be of what one day we shall do. Let our vow to the Lord be of what we shall do here and now — today. Let's make a beginning. The collection comes after the sermon to enable us to make an immediate response — albeit a token one — to the love of God made free to us in the Gospel. In the old days, in conveying land, a handful of the earth was actually handed over. In handing over the obedience of our wills and lives, we do well to make an immediate down-payment. — "They will make vows to the Lord — and perform them." For checking of our own fleeting emotion, for the purifying of our lives, for the undergirding of our feeble wills, for the sake of helping others and for the service of God, let us vow our vows — as members of the Church, as husband and wife, as parents. In our joys and in our sorrows, in our fears and longings, let us make our vows to the Lord, and, having vowed, let us perform our vows, resting on the everlasting mercy of God in Jesus Christ.

For the centre, the core, the secret of our religion is not a rigid law nor a resolute will, but a Person, the Person of Jesus Christ. Close to Him, all things become possible. Without Him our lives are failing and paltry. Only if we abide in Him will Isaiah's prophesy be true of us, "They will make vows to the Lord — and perform them."

Stand Tall

Ezekiel 2.1 (RSV) "Son of man, stand upon your feet."

Professor Roland Bainton's great biography of Martin Luther is called *Here I Stand*. The title is taken from Luther's majestic declaration which was a landmark in the progress of the Reformation. He said, "Here stand I, so help me God. I can do no other."

In the Church of Scotland when men and women are admitted as communicant members, they are required, not to kneel, but to stand in their places as their names are read. There is much to be said for the custom.

In the first place, it represents a pinning of their colours to the mast, a declaration of loyalty for all to see. As each stands, he or she is declaring his or her allegiance to Christ. A phrase which is much used these days is "Stand up and be counted". And that is what the new members are doing, enlisting in the army of Christ. In the everlasting fight between good and evil, between right and wrong, between truth and falsehood, between love and hate, they are declaring, as we all declare when we stand with them, that we stand for good and right and truth and love. As the familiar hymn has it, "Stand up, stand up for Jesus, Ye soldiers of the Cross".

With so much of sheer evil in the world — violence, cruelty, deceit, lust, theft — it is no time for Christ's folk to be neutral.

It is time for us to declare where we stand and to stand there. Those who do not stand for something in a world such as ours, will stand for anything. We have no right to be impartial as between good and evil, or agnostic when faced with the choice between truth and falsehood. We are all being confronted with the same choice as that with which Joshua confronted the Children of Israel, "Choose this day whom you will serve". We cannot postpone the choice any longer, nor evade the issue.

Many of us who are older learned, when we were at school, J. R. Lowell's little poem:

"Once to every man and nation comes the moment to decide,
In the strife of truth with falsehood, for the good or evil side.
Some great cause, God's new Messiah, offering each the
bloom or blight,
Parts the goats upon the left hand and the sheep upon the right,
And the choice goes by forever twixt that darkness and that
light."

So God gives us grace to obey when we hear His command, "Son of man, stand upon your feet".

Secondly, it is right that we should all stand before God, because standing is the appropriate preliminary to taking action. Christianity is not only a matter of declaring our loyalty, of standing with Christ, but of doing something about it. When soldiers are given a command, they are first of all called to stand to attention. It is unthinkable that they should receive their orders sitting down. That is why we stand to receive the blessing at the end of the service. We are being dismissed into the world to the obedience and service of Christ. When the risen Christ appeared to Peter, He asked him three times, "Simon, son of Jonas, do you love me?" When to each question Peter answered "Yes", Christ did not say "That is good", or even "I love you too". After each confession of Peter's love, Christ gave him a command, "Feed my sheep", or "Feed my lambs".

The final criterion by which our lives will be judged is not by the frequency of our cries of "Lord, Lord", nor yet by the depths of our emotions, but by what we do. "I was hungry and you gave me food, I was thirsty and you gave me drink, . . . I was naked and you clothed me, I was sick and you visited me, I was in prison and you came to me." "Come, O blessed of my Father, inherit the kingdom prepared for you from the foundation of the world."

Sons and daughters of man, stand upon your feet.

1. As a declaration of loyalty.
2. As a preliminary to action; and
3. As a mark of respect for yourselves.

What we owe to every other member of the human race, every other member of the family of God, is respect; and we shall respect others only if we respect ourselves. God made man in His own image. That is our origin. We are made like the Most High God. No matter if the image is obscured or even shattered; as we were, as we are, Christ thought we were worth dying for, and His desire is that we shall be fitted to live with Him for ever. St John is quite clear what God's ultimate purpose is for each one of us. "See what love the Father has given us, that we should be called children of God" — "We are God's children now; it does not yet appear what we shall be, but we know that when he appears we shall be like him, for we shall see him as he is." With such a sublime origin and such an august destiny, I dare not despise myself or others.

One of the States of the United States is known as the "Whoseyer State". It is said that people there are always asking "Who's your father?" — a silly enough question in all conscience, but, as far as we are concerned, there is but one reply we can give to that question. We should give it with our heads held high, "My Father is God". If that is so, we need not grovel in self-abasement before anyone.

Sons and daughters of man, stand upon your feet, declaring

your loyalty to God, in readiness to serve His purposes, and in the knowledge of the ineradicable dignity and honour He has conferred upon us all.

Above all, stand in the assurance of the totally undeserved and limitless love he has shown us in Jesus Christ.

We should honour ourselves and all people, for the Son of God was content to be as we are, clothed in the same flesh. He was tempted in all points like as we are, knew our sorrows, suffered our pain, died our death; and from the other side of that death, He summons us to declare our loyalty to Him, to give ourselves to His service, to accept the new dignity He has conferred upon every one of us.

No matter who you are or what, no matter what you've done or been, clever or foolish, rich or poor, black or white, leave the church with your head held high. You are stamped plain with the image of the King. Princes and Princesses, you bear the likeness of your Father, the Most High God. He will accept your loyalty. He will use your service. By His grace, He will make you at last fit to live with Him for ever. We may be formed out of the dust of the earth, born as "a wild ass's colt", but Jesus Christ has made us kings and priests to His God and Father. To Him be glory and dominion for ever and ever.

"Son of man, stand upon your feet."

COMMUNION

Hands

Luke 9.44 (RSV) "The Son of man is to be delivered into the hands of men."

What an extraordinary thing the human hand is; how delicate in movement, how ingenious in construction, how adaptable to tasks as varied as threading a needle, grasping a sledge hammer, writing a letter, building a house, playing a violin, or performing one of the thousands tasks we ask of it every day.

How expressive too of the emotions the hand is — the open hand of the generous, the grasping hand of the greedy, the outturned hand of prohibition, the beckoning hand of encouragement. Nothing so reveals a person's mood or even nature as the movements of his or her hands — the in-turned fist of anger, the threatening fist, the soothing hand of the mother, the healing hand of the doctor or nurse. In some ways hands are the most distinctively human parts of our body — so cruel they can be and so kind, so able to help, so ready to hurt.

And it was into the hands of men that the Son of Man was delivered that they might do with Him as they would.

Think of those who had Christ in their hands in the last few days of His life.

There were the hands of Judas who betrayed Him — hands reaching out for thirty pieces of silver.

Well, here we are all Christian people at Communion. We have nothing in common with Judas. But he was at the first Communion. Have none of us ever preferred money to Christ, betrayed Him by dishonesty or greed? Look at your hands. Could they ever be as the hands of Judas?

From the hands of Judas, Jesus was delivered into the hands

149

of Pilate. He was not a bad chap — a civil servant, determined to avoid trouble for himself, but with no real evil in him and a good judge. The man Jesus was clearly innocent, but the crowd were in an ugly mood and so water was brought and Pilate washed his hands of Him.

Surely we cannot be accused of the cool indifference that Pilate showed? I wonder. Have we never kept quiet when we should have spoken? Have we never betrayed Christ by refusing to be involved? Have we never said "It's up to them" — the ministers or elders or police? "It's not our responsibility." Look at your hands. They're clean. Is it because you've washed your hands of Christ — like Pilate, and so let Christ be delivered to those who would crucify Him, and soldiers who smote Him with the palms of their hands and who finally drove in the nails?

At least this we could not do. Yet Jesus once said, "As you did it to one of the least of these my brethren, you did it to me". Have we never made the innocent suffer — our children, our parents, our wives, our husbands, our relatives, our friends? What of the cruel things we have said to them and about them, the bitter quarrels about little or nothing, the disputes about money? What of those dying of hunger because we do not care? Which is worse — to crucify Christ or to starve Him to death?

Look at your hands. Could they be the hands of those who have crucified Christ anew in His brethren?

There were other hands that touched Our Lord. There were the hands of Mary, who anointed Him with the box of spikenard, in her overflowing love. Can we think of one wildly extravagant thing we have done for Christ? There were the hands of Simon of Cyrene who carried His cross. Do we daily lighten the load Christ carried? There were the hands of Joseph of Arimathea — a rich man but a good and a just, who with his own hands wrapped the body of Jesus and laid it in a new tomb, taking his stand with the Crucified, putting his own reputation, and even safety, at risk.

Today a piece of bread will be given to each of us, and a little wine. As we receive them, we receive Christ into our hands, to do with Him what we will. We won't put the bread on the floor and stamp on it, but there are ways in which we could hurt Him more. His cause, His kingdom, His reputation will depend on how we behave, what we say and do and are in the days that lie ahead.

Shall we betray Him like Judas, or wash our hands of Him like Pilate or crucify Him anew? Or shall we offer him our best, like Mary, and help to carry the dread burden laid upon Him like Simon, and like Joseph, take our stand with Him, at risk to our own reputation and when all seems lost? Where do we stand? With Judas, Pilate and the soldiers or with Mary, Simon and Joseph? We must choose.

The fact that we are here proves nothing. Remember the words of Christ, "Behold the hand of him who betrays me is with me *on the table*. . .woe to that man by whom he is betrayed."

Can the hands that receive the Bread of Life betray the Lord of Life? This is sure. The Son of man *is* delivered into the hands of men — into your hands and mine.

———————— · ————————

Remembrance

1 Corinthians 11.24, 26 (RSV) "Do this in remembrance of me . . . for as often as you eat this bread and drink this cup, you proclaim the Lord's death until he comes."

The Lord's Supper is rooted and grounded in history. It looks back to a real event, to Jesus of Nazareth who was born and lived and died and rose in Palestine, 1900 years ago. Its prime purpose is remembrance. He who knew the human heart as no one else ever did, knew that among the disciples in the Upper Room, all but Judas' hearts beat loyally. But He knew too how quickly men forget. It is so easy to make great promises — as Peter did — when danger is remote, so easy when the crunch comes to say, "I never knew the man." So, knowing the frailty of the disciples and our frailty, Christ instituted the Supper. "Come together often", He said, "and remember me." And as if in answer to their unspoken question, "But how shall we, if you are not there with us?", He said, "Let the bread and wine stand in place of me." So it has been that ever since, where His disciples have gathered together to remember Christ, the bread and wine have acted as symbols for the Lord whom we cannot see. And through all the years that lie between then and now, not a week has passed, scarcely a day, in which somewhere in the world, this Supper has not been celebrated.

Nearly 1400 years ago, near this spot, St Blane first read the very words we shall hear and broke the bread and took the cup, as the savage Picts looked curiously on. Six hundred years passed and this Cathedral was at last completed. If we could be transported back to the first service, everything but the building itself would be unfamiliar. There would be incense and candles and gorgeously robed priests, and no music but the human voice. Everything would seem strange until the priest came to the reading of 1 Corinthians and took bread and wine in his hands.

As we take these same symbols, we are joining in the one Supper, ages old and worldwide, which began in the Upper Room, and with Christians of every age and place we are remembering Christ as He wished to be remembered.

But if remembrance of the Jesus who lived so long ago had been the only meaning of the Lord's Supper, it would have ceased long since and all trace of the Christian faith would have perished with it. This has not happened because Christ, whose death we remember, rose again and is as alive now as on the first Easter Day. This is the explanation of the curious vitality of the Lord's Supper. It is not the morbid commemoration of a murder. It is a meeting with a friend. It is not a dead man we recall, but the living Christ with whom we meet — as alive today and as present here as when He walked and talked and healed and helped in Galilee.

At first sight it might seem monstrously irrelevant to gather here to eat a little bread and to drink a little wine amidst the grim realities of our world. And it *is* monstrously irrelevant if all we do is to eat the bread and drink the wine. But at every Communion we pray that the Holy Spirit may come among us and into our hearts, so that the bread and wine may no longer be merely bread and wine but may be, to our faith, as the very body and blood of our crucified and risen Lord. If that miracle happens, as I believe it always does, then the Sacrament is relevant to the desperate need of our tortured and war-torn world. Indeed, it is the only thing that is adequate to the desperate need of our own hearts and lives, for it tells of the compassion of God and of His mighty help, freely available to us. And nothing less than the help of God is adequate to our needs.

Certainly, if there is no help from beyond, if there be no God, or if that God be powerless or unwilling to help, there is no escape from despair. But, as Christ Himself gives into our hands the bread and wine which are the symbols of His perfect and complete sacrifice, He assures us that He is able to do exceedingly abundantly above all that we can ask or think, and that He is willing. These symbols tell of a love that sets no limits, and of a power that admits no bounds.

Through all the ages, the Communion has brought comfort and courage and hope to sore-burdened men and women, not because of some magic in the bread and wine, but because at the Communion they have met with Christ — Christ crucified but risen, and have known that He is able to save to the uttermost those who put their trust in Him.

Yet, of course, there is an imperfection about life's most

perfect moments, a necessary imperfection which leaves us longing still. However real our Communion, there are great unsolved questions in life — Why pain? Why sorrow? Why death? What's beyond? So the Lord's Supper is not only remembrance of what is past, not only a present experience of the Living Christ, but is promise and foretaste of the better and the best which is to be.

Remembrance — how much that means.

Communion — how much that helps.

But both mock us unless lit up by a boundless hope.

Memory; Communion; hope. Of these life is made up. And of these our Holy Faith speaks in the Lord's Supper.

Remembrance of Christ.

Communion with Christ.

Hope in Christ.

In the Lord's Supper we receive nothing less, nothing other than Christ Himself. And He is sufficient for now — and for ever.

Jesus said, "Do this in remembrance of me."

All Shall Be Well

Romans 8.38-39 (RSV) "I am sure that neither death, nor life, nor angels, nor principalities, nor things present, nor things to come, nor powers, nor height, nor depth, nor anything else in all creation, will be able to separate us from the love of God in Christ Jesus our Lord."

I've never felt in the least inclined to rail at those who come to Holy Communion and who are not often there in between times. Of course, it would be wonderful if everybody were to be in church every Sunday, but far better sometimes — even if not very frequently — than never. It's only because we know that Christ is always glad to welcome sinners that any one of us dare come at all.

What is interesting is that those who come, or perhaps *can* come only occasionally to church, choose generally to come to the Lord's Supper. I wonder why. The cynical would give all sorts of reasons. I spoke to one dear old man one Sunday and said, "I'm glad you managed to get to church today." With great frankness he replied, "I might not have been if I hadn't had a great pile of envelopes to hand in!" Others, inclined to judge their neighbours, might say these folk come from sheer habit, or from the desire to be with the crowd, or from the wish to have their attendance recorded. There is something in all of these suggestions, no doubt, for we are all feeble, earthy creatures.

But there is something else, something deeper, something profoundly spiritual and very real. There is something here which has enabled this frail craft of the Lord's Supper to survive all the tempests of fierce persecution, the centuries of turmoil and periods of radical revolution, of political cataclysm and economic change. Empires have flourished and disappeared, vast movements of population have taken place, inventions have altered our whole lives, but the Holy Communion continues. Two hundred years after the French Revolution and 75 years after the Russian Revolution had tried to abolish all religious services, the Lord's Supper is still being celebrated in the centre of Paris and Moscow today. Yes, and in Peking and Havana too.

Amidst all the mighty movements which have rocked our world, this very simple service continues in the precise form laid down in the Bible, with no alteration in its essentials. No attempt has ever been made to adapt it to the changing styles and circumstances by which it is surrounded. What is the explanation of the almost incredible survival of the Lord's Supper?

The explanation, the only possible explanation, is that

somehow, contained within, behind, beyond and beneath these material things — the crumb of bread and the sip of wine so quickly consumed, so transient — that in and under them is something — no, rather someone, eternal, unchanged and unchangeable. It is this eternal core which gives the Lord's Supper its perennial vitality.

The truth is that whether they have been aware of it or not, people throughout the ages have found Christ in the Sacrament or been found by Him.

Christ is the origin of the Sacrament.

Christ is the meaning of the Sacrament.

Christ is the object of the Sacrament.

It has no other purpose nor intention but to bring each one of us nearer to Him. As the bread and wine — the symbols of our earthiness — become irreversibly part of our bodies, of our very tissues, so Christ Himself comes to nourish our souls. As something of the bread and wine will forever remain part of our flesh, so nothing will ever completely separate us from the Christ who comes to us as we accept the symbols of His love.

At the closing session of the General Assembly, the retiring Moderator reads out, in accordance with long custom, the names of all the ministers who have died in the 12 months since the last Assembly. It is a solemn occasion as one recognises the names of colleagues one has known all one's life, and as one realises anew that one day one's own name will be read.

One year, from where I sat, I could see a minister's widow whom I knew, whose husband had died recently. When her husband's name was read, she gave a gentle sob and her tears began to flow. The Moderator gave his closing address then, and in the course of it told a little story of a French priest who noticed how often a certain peasant came to the church and stayed for shorter or longer periods. One day the priest asked him what he did when he was in church. "Well," said the peasant, pointing to the image of Christ on the crucifix, "I just sit and look at Christ and he looks at me." I look at Him and He looks at me. As she listened to the little story, the widow regained her composure and dried her tears. So we came to the closing paraphrase, the words of our text:

"The Saviour died, but rose again
Triumphant from the grave;
And pleads our cause at God's right hand,
Omnipotent to save."

As we came to the eighth verse, my eyes rested on the widow again and the brave soul lifted her head and with all her heart sang:

"Nor death, nor life, nor earth, nor hell,
Nor time's destroying sway,
Can e'er efface us from his heart
Or make his love decay."

That's what the Sacrament is all about. Look at Christ and let Christ look at you — and be at peace.

There are perplexities and perils in the world. There are sorrows and disappointments and terrors in our own lives, but nothing can cut us off from the love of God. Nothing can weary, nothing can defeat the Conqueror of death, and all He has and all He is, is ours. As proof of that, take the bread and drink the cup.

"This is my body", said Christ. "This is my blood poured forth." This is all of me there is and without reserve, without condition I give myself to you.

"I am sure that neither death, nor life, nor angels, nor principalities, nor things present, nor things to come, nor powers, nor height, nor depth, nor anything else in all creation, will be able to separate us from the love of God in Christ Jesus our Lord."

As Julian of Norwich wrote, "*All* shall be well. All *shall* be well and all manner of thing shall be well."

Don't doubt it, my friends. Don't doubt it.

———— · ————

Bread

Matthew 15.34 (NEB) "'How many loaves have you?' Jesus asked."

Much attention has been paid to the feeding of the 4000 and little heed to the curious fact that, before He could begin, Christ needed something from the crowd. To the disciples this must have seemed a foolish question. There were four thousand people to be fed. Half a ton of bread would not be enough and Jesus asked, "How many loaves have you?" "Seven," they replied, "and there are a few small fishes" — a boy 's lunch piece, not worth speaking about. But Christ asked and they answered, and finally Christ used what they had to accomplish His good purpose. No doubt He could have fed the people some other way. But He chose to use what little they could offer.

So, in a curious way, the first thing we do in the Sacrament, is not to receive but to offer what we can offer. We buy the bread and wine and, before the Supper, we bring the collection and then the bread and wine and offer them to Christ on His table for His acceptance.

God always deals with His children in this way. No doubt the fields could yield crops by His simple command, but He has chosen that we should sow a handful of seed. No doubt He could have chosen to heal our diseases without our help, but He has chosen to use the doctor and the nurse. No doubt He could overpower our minds and storm our hearts, but He prefers to wait till we offer our little stock of faith before He marvellously multiplies it to our use. On Whitsunday, when the Holy Spirit came in power upon the pathetic handful of frightened disciples, before even the Spirit could work the miracle of the creation of the Church, the few disciples had to gather with their prayers.

"How many loaves have you?"

Yet, of course, there is a vast disproportion between the

seven loaves and a few small fishes, and food for 4000 hungry people. Without Christ's blessing, it is a hopelessly inadequate provision. What a foolish thing the Sacrament may seem — eating a little bread and drinking a little wine — how foolish unless Christ be there to heal and to bless. How little is what we offer compared with what we receive. A few loaves of bread, a few bottles of wine are offered, but after the Sacrament has been celebrated, hundreds of men and women will go forth, their sorrows comforted, their anxieties stilled, their faith strengthened, their burdens lightened and their resolve renewed to live more cleanly, more rightly, more kindly.

Of course, we bring something more than just bread and wine to the Sacrament. We bring some little love for Christ, some little longing for God, else we would not come to the Holy Table. God accepts these too — our handful of doubts, our few bits of service, some minor temptations conquered, a little hesitant faith and a desire to do and to be better.

And there will be baskets of the fragments that remain. The Sacrament is for our own spiritual nourishment, for the feeding of our souls; but not for us only. It should be the inspiration for us to serve our fellows better. Christian Aid reminds us of the need of the world for bread, and we who eat of the Bread of God cannot be content so long as any of His other children are hungry — and millions of them are.

But the need of men and women is not for bread alone. Sometimes our world seems to be coming apart. The situation in Ulster, the violence in our streets, drug and alcohol addiction, the rampant materialism of society — these come, not from lack of bread, but from lack of faith and hope and love. We may feel that we have not enough of these for ourselves, but if we share what we have, we *shall* have enough. The more we give, the more we will have for ourselves. And what we have we must offer — not just our money, but our gifts and talents, the service we can render, the influence, however slight, we can exert.

With no false pride and with no false shame, let us bring forth what we have and, with no holding back, offer it for the blessing of Christ, that His miracle may be wrought anew. To each of us, as to His disciples, he speaks, "How many loaves have you?"

THANKSGIVING AFTER COMMUNION

Take; Offer; Pay

We are met in thanksgiving tonight. How shall we show our gratitude? The Psalmist suggests three ways, but first he asks the question, in Psalm 116.12 (NEB) "How can I repay the Lord for all his gifts to me?" His three answers are:

"I will take."

"I will offer."

"I will pay my vows to the Lord."

We have all been in the position of being greatly obliged to someone, of being at a loss to know how we can show our gratitude. That is how the Psalmist feels. He is thinking of what God has done for him. "Be at rest once more, my heart, for the Lord has showered gifts upon you. He has rescued me from death and my feet from stumbling." Remembering all that God has done for him, the Psalmist feels he must find some way of repaying God for all His goodness to him.

So may we each of us feel, for we have been given so much. Life itself, and life is very sweet; a Godly upbringing; particular benefits — temptations resisted which could easily have brought us to shame, dreams turned into reality, even the dews of sorrow lustred by God's love. And sometimes — as at Communion — hints of another dimension of life and the knowledge of a mystery which is, all love.

Well may we echo the Psalmist's cry, "How can I repay the Lord for all his gifts to me?"

The first answer of the Psalmist is full of commonsense. "I will take." He accepts what God has to offer and accepts it gladly.

There is no merit in misery. We should enjoy what is to be enjoyed in life — a good meal, a comfortable home, good friends, happy memories, the beauty and grandeur of nature, books and music, sport and laughter. All of these we should accept, and much else, as tokens of God's Love itself. This is the great point of the Sacrament. At the Communion we are not doing or serving or giving. We are taking, accepting the unconditional, unearned, unlimited love of God, made free to us, and the first duty we owe to God is to accept that love, and to accept all He gives, with thanksgiving.

Yet, if once we know that all we enjoy comes from the hand of God, we cannot grudge to give. So, if the Psalmist's first response to God's goodness is to take, his second response is to offer. "To Thee will I bring a thank-offering", and by that he meant not only saying but doing something.

Since God has given us food, clothing, shelter, comforts aplenty, we ought not to grudge Him anything He asks. Of course, He Himself needs nothing from us, but He has appointed a surrogate — someone to receive from us payment of the debt we owe. "Anything you did for one of my brothers here, however humble, you did for me." So long as one child in the world is hungry, Christ is hungry. So long as one is thirsty or naked or imprisoned or homeless, Christ is thirsty or naked or imprisoned or homeless.

It is not only food and clothing and shelter we owe. Men and women have other needs. They cannot live by bread alone. If the Gospel of God's love in Christ has met the need of our hungry souls, we cannot be content until all the world has heard the Good News. The population of the world increases by over 60 million a year and most of those will live and die with no knowledge of the Love of God in Christ unless we bestir ourselves to offer in response what we have received.

"How can I repay the Lord for all his gifts to me?"

"I will take", "I will offer", and

"I will pay my vows to the Lord in the presence of all his people."

Most of us at the Communion remember the vows that once

we made when we became church members. We remember too, with shame, how ill we have kept them — how casual have been our prayers, how imperfect our service, how grudging our obedience. But the perseverance of the saints is made up of a series of new beginnings, and every Communion should be a new beginning for us all.

"I will pay my vows to the Lord in the presence of all his people." Why in the presence of all His people? Would it not be enough to make our vows to the Lord in the secret places of our own hearts? Why make a parade of our loyalty? To that there are two answers. First that the open and public profession of faith strengthens it. The human heart is "deceitful above all things and desperately wicked" — our inward resolves are apt to melt away, to be brushed aside by the first passing sleeve unless we declare them. The second reason is that the only way in which we can put our faith to work, is by declaring it, and the Bible knows nothing of an unproductive faith — one for private enjoyment only. Christ has made no other provision for the growth of His Kingdom than the words and lives of those whom He has already called.

God is merciful and may have His own gracious plans for those who — like Nicodemus — are disciples only secretly, for fear of men. That we cannot know. But surely the response of honest men and women to the goodness of God as it was revealed in Christ, is not only to take what is given, but to share it, and in response to vow anew the loyalty of their hearts and the obedience of their surrendered wills.

So let us now, in the secret of our hearts and in the days to come by our words and by our lives, witness to the grace by which we have been saved.

"How can I repay the Lord for all his gifts to me?"

"I will take."

"I will offer."

"I will pay my vows to the Lord in the presence of all his people."

SERMONS FOR OTHER SUNDAYS

THE CHURCH

Is God in There?
(The place of the Church building)

1 Kings 8.27 (NEB) "But can God indeed dwell on earth? Heaven itself, the highest heaven, cannot contain thee; how much less this house that I have built."

Solomon certainly thought that a great and beautiful church was a help to worship, else he would not have poured forth his wealth so prodigally on building the great Temple at Jerusalem. Yet, he was a man aware of danger, and so he asks this searching question, "Can God indeed dwell on earth?" And he gave the answer, "Heaven itself, the highest heaven cannot contain Thee; how much less this house that I have built." God cannot be shut up in a building, however fine.

A former Bishop of Woolwich announced in *Honest to God* that God was not located in any one place. True enough. The Shorter Catechism has been teaching that for over 300 years. "God is a spirit, infinite, eternal and unchangeable in His being, wisdom, power, holiness, justice, goodness and truth." Our fathers knew that God was a most pure spirit without body, parts or passions. Five thousands years ago the Jews knew it. They put the cherubim on either side of the Ark of the Covenant, but the centre place was empty, with no representation of God. It is He that "Sits throned on the vaulted roof of earth, whose inhabitants are like grasshoppers. He stretches out the skies like a curtain, he spreads them out like a tent to live in." "Heaven itself, the highest heaven, cannot contain thee."

"Is God in there?" a small boy once asked, standing outside a church. "Yes," said his father. "Let's see Him," said the little boy. This is all we want — to cut God down to size, our size.

This is the temptation to idolatry — to take something we can handle and control and say, "This shall be our God." It does not much matter whether it be the Wafer God, or the Bible God, or the Sunday God. If it be any other god than the Lord God whom the highest heaven cannot contain, it is an idol.

There is no idolatry more common than that of the church — to take a building and worship it in place of God. This is what makes the necessary task of church union so slow and tedious. Men and women worship stone and lime. While a lovely church can be a help to the worship of God, it can also be a temptation. Solomon knew the human heart when, at the dedication of his Temple, he cried, "Heaven itself, the highest heaven, cannot contain thee; how much less this house that I have built?"

If God is not to be contained in any house, why do we build churches at all — 200 in Scotland since the war, at a cost of millions of pounds? Is it all a waste of money? Yes! if by the building of churches the notion has been encouraged that God lives only in churches, leaving the world to go its hell-ward way. The field of God's activity and concern is the world — the world of men and affairs — of Ulster, deprivation, drug addiction, AIDS and the crime rate. We cannot confine God to one day of the week, nor to one segment of our affairs, nor to a special kind of building. "Can God indeed dwell on the earth? Heaven itself, the highest heaven, cannot contain thee; how much less this house."

And yet, we are not disembodied spirits. A wedding ring is not a few pounds worth of gold. It is a symbol of all that marriage means. The flag is not only a piece of coloured cloth. It expresses our love of our country, and people have died for it. The water, the bread and the wine cost practically nothing, but they speak of the Grace of God which is beyond cost. We need symbolism in our religion and places set apart. Although God does not need a church, *we* do. God is everywhere, but it is not equally easy for us to draw near Him everywhere. When we turn on a tap, the whole waterworks does not rush into our home, but as much as we need does. While God does not live in a church, we draw upon His grace there, there find the tiny portion of His mighty strength that we need. We must have a place of prayer where in quietness we can offer our worship and hear God's Word and receive His Sacraments. We need a place set apart.

There are two movements in the Christian symphony. There is the outward thrust into the world — the work of mission, of evangelism, the claiming of all God's world for God's obedience. But if we honestly try to obey God in such a world as ours, we shall often be driven to the secret place of God's abiding for renewal and refreshment. During the war, naval ships used to come to the Holy Loch to check their compasses. We all need our Holy Loch in the midst of the stresses and storms of life. Those who come to a church, large or humble, seeking God, will not be sent empty away. For the God whom the highest heaven cannot contain, nor any place of worship, however great or lovely, has poured Himself into the one human life of Jesus of Nazareth. Still God comes in Christ, as at the first, wherever He can find one humble heart or home in which to dwell.

"Can God indeed dwell on earth?" asked Solomon. "The Word became flesh — to dwell among us", answered John. The miracle for which Solomon longed happened in Christ. God dwelt on the earth.

Every church was built for one purpose and one purpose only, and every church is worth maintaining only so long as this purpose is being served — that the God whom the highest heaven cannot contain may there meet with ordinary folk. And so He does, and so He shall, for we have Christ's promise that "Where two or three have met together in my name, I am there among them." And so He is. It is all there. "Can God indeed dwell on earth?" "Where two or three have gathered together in my name, I am there among them."

Lo I Am With You
(The place of the Church services)

Let us take three words — literally three words — of Our Lord. They are words He used, not once, but many times. Together they sum up the life which is in Christ.
"COME." "Abide." "GO."
And let us take three texts from the Revised Standard Version which are typical.
Matthew 11.28 "Come to me, all who labour and are heavy laden, and I will give you rest."
John 15.4 "Abide in me."
Luke 9.60 "Go and proclaim the kingdom of God."

Why do you leave a comfortable home to walk or drive to church, to spend an hour sitting on very hard and uncomfortable pews, singing hymns you don't always mean, listening to scriptures you don't always understand, hearing sermons which are sometimes as stale as a twice told tale, over the whole affair a faint air of unreality, or irrelevance to the workday world of tomorrow?

Well, some would say that the Church is maybe irrelevant when things are going along quite nicely, thank you, but they add darkly, "You never know when you may need the Church", implying that the Church and the Church's Lord and Church's ministry are a kind of celestial fire-brigade, doing nothing for much of the time but ready to be called out when an emergency arises — death, disaster, grave illness or some sort of family or marriage crisis.

There is a certain amount of truth in this attitude. Assuming that this week is going to hold for you just the usual quota of work and play, minor irritations and tiny pleasures which most weeks hold, then you could probably get through it in much the same way whether you have been to Church or not. Habit and routine are great things and carry us through most days, without our ever having to ask ourselves whether life is worth living or not, whether it has meaning or not.

If your wife or your husband are reasonably well and your children are normal, if you have enough to pay the grocer and even sometimes the butcher, it is possible to manage fairly well without religion. As Laplace once said to Napoleon, speaking of God, "Sir, I have no need of the hypothesis." If people say they have no need of God, we must just leave them to it. Argument is profitless. We must just wait for the reproofs of life. The soundness of a house is not discovered on a calm and sunny afternoon but only when the rains descend and the floods rise and the winds blow. It is then that the difference between the house built on sand and that built on rock becomes apparent.

Those who refuse to be taught by words are sooner or later taught by life, are forced to admit that life is too big for them:

"Lips cry 'God be merciful'
That ne'er cried 'God be praised'."

There are few lives that are not touched by tragedy sooner or later — sorrow, moral failure, faithlessness of a partner, loss of work or health or both. When these great challenges of life appear, we know our own insufficiency and the great questions press in upon us — is there meaning in life; is there a God who cares; is there life after death? When these questions are no longer a matter of airy-fairy theory but of vital importance, when we are bruised and battered by life and can hardly keep our feet, then Christ's words hold our only hope — "Come to me, all who labour and are heavy laden."

These traumatic experiences which drive us to Christ are often the beginning of a relationship that lasts all through life. The Reformation in Germany began, not with a meeting of a Council or the report of a committee. It began on a sultry day in 1505, when a young student at the University of Erfurt was struck to the ground by lightning and was driven by the dreadful experience into the arms of God. A great many people have been brought to Christ by the occasion when they had no one else to turn to. And Christ does not drive such desperate souls away. He never did in his life in Palestine and He does not now. This for many is the beginning of it all but not the end.

But life is not all crises — happily. Mostly it is just ordinary and it is its very ordinariness which often wears us down. It is the steady erosion of daily work and worry and frustration and irritation. People who face death without flinching become petulant when faced with toothache or a sink full of dirty dishes.

I have run through a fair number of motor cars. Not one has been destroyed in some spectacular accident. All have finally succumbed to what is called "Fair wear and tear". That is what leaves us played out and exhausted so often at the end of the week — fair wear and tear.

Which is why we need not only to come to Christ in our moments of great need, but to abide in Him from day to day. Sunday morning service should be a weekly time of refreshment and renewal, a recovery of our breath, a healing of the bruises and scratches of the week before. Every Sunday is a great occasion. Sometimes the music is better than at other times; sometimes the sermon is worse than at other times. But always I have the feeling of "occasion" on a Sunday morning in church. This is the high point of my week, to be prepared for, agonised over and prayed for — and sometimes repented of.

I like to think that for many of you it is the occasion of the week too — a time when an opening is made in our humdrum lives through which Eternity may be glimpsed, an occasion never without some thrill of wonder, some reaching out beyond the seen and temporal to the unseen Lord of Life, so that our souls, fretted and wearied by the chances and changes of this fleeting world, may find repose in Christ and come to abide in Him.

To come to Christ.

To abide in Him.

But Christ's third, Christ's last word is "Go." We are called not only to come to Christ and to abide in Him, but in His name to go back to the world for which He died and to serve Him there. We are called by Christ not for comfort and strengthening only, but to service. We are asked not just to hold to Him, but to rise to the challenge of life, to advance the kingdom of God.

Christ said of the Church that the Gates of Hell shall not prevail against it. No text has been more misunderstood. It is nearly always taken to mean that an embattled Church, besieged in a fortress, will always be able to fight off the attacks of the infidel. That may be true but it is not what Christ said. He said that an embattled hell in an apparently impregnable fortress would not be able to fight off the attack of Christ and His Church. Christ gave us a strategy, not of defence, but of attack. "Go therefore," He said, "and make disciples of all nations." "You shall be my witnesses in Jerusalem and in all Judea and Samaria and to the end of the earth."

We have the answer for which the world, the world of Africa and Lebanon and Ulster, is crying out, for the answer is Christ. That answer we should be proclaiming, not with arrogance, but with assurance and conviction.

"Come to me," said Christ.

"Abide in me,"

and for my sake and the Gospel's, "Go and proclaim the kingdom of God."

Who is able for such things? To close with Christ and face the great crises of life? To abide with Christ and so face the daily erosion of our strength and to go and share what we have found in Him with all our brethren of mankind? Who is able for this? Not one of us in our own strength. Fortunately we don't need to depend on our own strength.

I said Christ's last word to us was "Go." That was not quite true. His last and blessed word is — "Lo." "Lo, I am with you always, to the close of the age."

Life is hard, sometimes very hard, but with Christ beside us
we may face it without flinching or fear, and by His help be of
some use to our hard-pressed brethren.

"Come to me," said Christ.

"Abide with me," said Christ.

"Go," said Christ.

"And Lo, I am with you always." So He is and so He will be
— to the end and beyond it for ever.

————————— · —————————

The Mustard Seed
(The growth of the Church)

Mark 4.30-31 "The kingdom of God — is like the mustard
seed — which grows."

Although we are apt to take it for granted, growth is a very
strange and wonderful thing. It happens only in living things
but in living things it never ceases.

It obviously fascinated Our Lord. "Consider" He said, not
"how they are," but "how they *grow*." "First the blade, then
the ear, then the full-grown corn in the ear." "A sower went
forth to sow." In the growth of the mustard seed to a great
tree, He saw a picture of the future growth of the Church.
That growth has been as spectacular as He predicted — scarce
a dozen when He died, there are now 1100 million Christians
in every continent. Every day there are 55,000 Christian
conversions throughout the world, mostly in Africa, South
America and the Far East. K. S. Latourette called his great
work *The History of the expansion of Christianity* and in it he
shows how the tide of religion has ebbed and flowed, with
advances and setbacks, but with each advance greater and
each setback less. It may be that here in Europe we have been
having something of a spiritual recession but the Church of

Christ is not the Church of one country or of one continent, but of the world, and we must take a world view.

> "For while the tired waves, vainly breaking
> Seem here no painful inch to gain,
> Far back through creek and inlet breaking
> Comes silent, flooding in, the main."

Even here there are signs of vitality. The Church of Scotland admits 250 new members every week. Any political party would be delighted to hear of such an accession of strength.

"The Kingdom of God is like the mustard seed — which grows."

But how does the great Church throughout the world grow and keep on growing and how will the Church of Scotland begin again to grow? The World Church is made up of congregations like ours, some of them quite small. For the Church to grow and keep on growing, each separate congregation must grow.

How can we make sure that this happens, make sure that our Church and our Congregation is part of the growing organism of the world-wide Church of Christ? There's only one way to ensure it. It is by being ourselves — growing Christians.

Are we? Are you and I growing in grace as the days and the years pass over us? Or were we baptised, went to Sunday School, Bible Class and First Communicants' Class — and then — finish. What should be the beginning of Christian discipleship — joining the Church, being confirmed — is very often the end. Too many of us are spiritual adolescents — believing what we've always believed, unadventurous in our prayers and timid in our service. It won't do. If our Christianity is not always growing it will die. Take any living thing, stop it growing and it will wither, and that is as true of our own souls as of our congregations and of our Church.

Just one other thing. There is no growth without sacrifice. The mustard seed becomes a tree only by dying itself. Christ said, "A grain of wheat remains a solitary grain unless it falls

into the ground and dies; but if it dies it bears a rich harvest."
Just so the Kingdom of God grows within us and in the world,
only by sacrifice. So it was founded and so has it spread. Growth
is a painful process and if we are to grow we must be ready day
by day for real sacrifice — of time and money, of pride and
prejudices, sacrifice of hoary traditions and old habits; and it
will hurt but it will be worth it if the miracle happens.

A great Scottish preacher of a past generation once asked his
people, "Do you believe your faith? If you do, you must believe
that one day you will stand before the throne of God and the
angels will say to each other 'How like he or she is to Christ'.
That is your faith." That may seem hard to believe but it should
not be. The God who can make a great tree grow from a tiny
seed can surely work a like miracle with the tiny seed of faith in
our souls — if only we let Him have His way with us.

"The kingdom of God is like the mustard seed — which
grows."

A growing Church to meet the needs of our exploding world.
Growing congregations within the World Church. Growing
Christians within the congregations. That is how it can be and
how it must be if we are to be true to those who went before
us and true above all to Him who by His own perfect sacrifice
pledged His all for us, who Himself said,

"The kingdom of God is like the mustard seed — which
grows."

———————— · ————————

Only One Thing is Necessary
(For the Church)

Luke 10.42 (NEB) "The part Mary has chosen is best."

I have the impression that most people, certainly most
housewives, have a good deal of sympathy with Martha. I

tried it out on the housewife I know best, whose reply was, "All right. If Mary is to be preferred to Martha, go and make the supper yourself!" So many would feel, suggesting that it was all very well for Mary to sit at Jesus' feet, drinking in every word, leaving poor Martha to get on with it in the kitchen.

But this is hardly fair. Mary was not a languid dreamer, sitting with folded hands, piously doing nothing. The translation in the Authorised Version gives the impression that she had already done her stint in the kitchen, but had been content to prepare one dish before sitting down to enjoy Jesus' company. Martha wanted to go one better, to put on a great spread. She was probably a splendid housekeeper, well known for her cooking, and here was an occasion to show what she could do. This was her way of showing her love of Christ.

But Jesus had set His face steadfastly to go to Jerusalem. The Cross was looming. The last thing that He wanted was a banquet. A very simple meal was all He desired. That is partly what He meant when He said, "but one thing is necessary." What He longed for was peace and quiet and the assurance of the loyalty and love of at least some of His friends. Mary sensed this and bringing the one dish of food, sat down to talk and to listen. Martha had become so interested in her great preparations that she was in danger of forgetting that the whole point of the preparations was the refreshment of Christ. Once the preparations became too elaborate or hectic, they defeated their own object. She became fussed and irritable and was even a bit querulous with her honoured guest.

It is a mistake we all can make. The wife and mother, determined to do her best for her children, drives herself harder and harder, taking on an extra job, cooking, cleaning every evening and every weekend, till she forgets the husband and children for whose sake she first began to put out such efforts, and like Martha, becomes a little peppery and plaintive. The good husband and father, determined to do his best for his wife and children, working seven days a week, doing overtime, moonlighting, all for the sake of his loved ones, but finally becoming such a workaholic as to deprive them of what they most need — his own company and attention. They both need to be reminded that "but one thing is necessary."

A habit common to most denominations of the Church is to have a major business meeting from time to time. The General Assembly of the Church of Scotland is one of them. I love the Assembly; its mixture of grandeur and homeliness; its bringing together of all the strands of our national life, of elders and ministers of parishes from the Shetlands to the Solway. The Assembly is, I think, the most truly democratic body in the world, for each one counts one and no more than one. Over the centuries an elaborate mechanism has grown up to ensure that the will of the whole Church shall be discovered and carried into effect. I love the dignity of the Assembly, its efficiency and order, its carefulness to protect the rights of every member.

Yet it has its danger — the danger of becoming so wrapped up in the mechanics of the thing as to forget what it is all about. Like Martha, the General Assembly, with, I suspect, most other similar gatherings, is very busy, very concerned and anxious, but has constantly to be reminded that the whole point and function of the Church is to bring men and women into a real relationship with God, to the feet of Christ. If that is not happening, the General Assembly, the Church of Scotland, this church and all its services are a meaningless charade. "But one thing is necessary." What we need is not bigger and better organisation but a revival of personal faith, a fresh understanding of Christ, a new response and allegiance to Him and an outpouring of the Holy Spirit.

The birthday of the Church is celebrated every year at Whitsunday. We need to be reminded that the Church was brought into being, not by an organisation nor by a committee nor even by a General Assembly. It was brought into being when the Holy Spirit came among twelve simple men and entered into the heart of each.

No doubt the structures of the Church have their uses — church buildings, offices, publishing houses, committees and the rest, but the power behind them all is what happens very quietly in the hearts of individual human beings and the point of it all is that that may happen all over again.

"He came sweet influence to impart
A gracious, willing guest,
While He can find one humble heart
Wherein to rest.
And His the gentle voice we hear,
Soft as the breath of even,
That checks each fault, that calms each fear,
And speaks of heaven."

The Holy Spirit is the one thing needed. If He be present, too elaborate organisation is not necessary. If He be not present, too elaborate organisation is completely pointless. "But one thing is necessary."

During the Assembly, there is always a focus on some of the consequences of the faith — disarmament, Christian Aid, homes for the elderly, laws to control pornography and many other things which grow from the Gospel. But if there be no living faith, the consequences will wither. Take the cut flowers from the vase on the Communion Table and stick them into the ground in the Manse garden and they will make a brave show for an hour or two, but by tomorrow morning they will have withered and died because they have no root. In the same way, the most elaborate schemes of the Church, the most careful drawing out of the results of the Gospel are useless if they are not rooted and grounded in a real and living faith in God through Jesus Christ.

The proclamation that there is a God — a God who is in all respects like Christ — is the Church's business, and that business depends not on structures but on personal experience. So, if Scotland and the world are to be won for Christ, as I believe that they can and pray that they will be, it will not be by church structures of increasing complexity, not by organisation nor by legislation. It will be by returning to a personal relationship with Christ. This is the heart of our faith on which all else depends.

What we need is a renewal of personal religion, a fresh response to Christ and a new allegiance to Him. Without this, nothing will help. From this, all else will follow.

Martha was distracted by her many tasks. Jesus said, "Martha, Martha, you are fretting and fussing about so many things; but one thing is necessary."

SUFFERING

The Problem of Evil

Job 2.10 (NEB) "If we accept good from God, shall we not accept evil?"

Evil, pain, suffering, are not problems where they are deserved. The glutton's dyspepsia, the drunkard's headache, the thief's term of imprisonment, are not problems even to those who suffer them. Nor is productive suffering a problem. The mother's pain in labour, the climber's pain as he battles with the bitter cold, the artist's pain as he struggles with his medium — these are productive evils, the necessary prelude to joy, for only that which is costing is really worth having.

The evil which is really a problem is that which is undeserved and unproductive, which does not follow on any misbehaviour, nor lead, so far as we can see, to any higher good. Why should a well-doing, industrious family have such bad luck? Why do some people have so much to suffer? This is the problem — the problem of seemingly sterile suffering — which teases the mind and torments the soul; and it is with this problem that the Book of Job is concerned. It deals with it by giving an account of an experiment which begins with a dialogue between God and Satan.

God is very proud of Job. He says to Satan, "Have you considered my servant Job? You will find no one like him on earth, a man of blameless and upright life, who fears God and sets his face against wrongdoing." But Satan is ready with a sneer and a smear, "Has not Job every reason to be God-fearing?" Job, he suggests, is only obedient to God for what he can get. God replies in effect, "I don't believe that, but go ahead and take everything — wealth, children, possessions, health, everything — and we'll see if Job's love is only cupboard-love or not." Satan takes God at His word and strips Job of everything. His oxen and asses are taken away by the Sabaeans and his servants slain. Lightning strikes his sheep and his shepherds. The Chaldaeans steal his camels. A hurricane destroys his house with his children in it. Finally his health goes. All he is left with is his wife, and she is not an unmixed blessing. She urges him to curse God and die. But Job will have none of it. "You talk as any fool of a woman might talk. If we accept good from God, shall we not accept evil?"

Evil at the hand of God — a strange thought. No other person has had the equal of Job's experience. He knew that the things that had happened to him — sorrow, sickness, loss — were evil. Yet equally he knew that these things had come from the hand of God. Even so, Job refuses to curse the God from whose hand such evil things had come. In the middle of his sufferings, Job fights for true religion — vindicating, as it were, the honour of God. He is certain that there is meaning and purpose in his suffering. But — and here is the point — Job does not know what the meaning and purpose are. He has not heard God's dialogue with Satan. He does not know — cannot know — why all the evil has come upon him; but, almost defiantly, he persists in his trust in God. The reader has been let into the secret of the experiment, but not Job. So, through pain and sorrow, he holds on to God in a bewildered kind of way, determined not to let Him go. "If we accept good from the hand of God, shall we not accept evil?"

This is religion at its purest and almost at its best. For the best and purest religion one has to wait for Jesus. For, if Gethsemane and the cry of dereliction mean anything, they mean that God's purpose in letting Him die is hidden from Jesus' eyes. And Jesus' faith is put to a further test than Job's — to the ultimate test, to the test of the Cross. And as He dies, He cries, "Father, into thy hands". "If we accept good from the hand of God, shall we not accept evil?"

Does this help us at all? Faced, as we often are, with

inexplicable pain and sorrow and loss for ourselves or — what is worse, perhaps — for others, can we not believe that there is a purpose, as there was for Job and for Jesus, which in the nature of the case cannot be disclosed to us? We often ask, "Why should this happen to me, or to her, or to him?" The answer to that kind of question we cannot have today or tomorrow, nor perhaps this side of heaven. But, if we believe in the God and Father of our Lord Jesus Christ, answer we shall have — and it will be an answer of love.

And meantime, when we lose something or someone we love, we need not also lose God. When we remember the sufferings of Christ, no one of us need feel deserted or alone in our own valley of the shadow. Christ is with us. Yes; and somehow, we with Him. As Peter said in one of his letters, "Do not be bewildered by the fiery ordeal — it gives you a share in Christ's sufferings, and that is cause for joy." Wherever there is sorrow borne with courage, or disappointment with cheerfulness, or pain without complaint, or defeat with dignity, there, as men and women stand with Christ, some part of the fearful burden resting on Him is shared by human hearts.

The purposes of God are often — perhaps mostly — hidden, but when they are most hidden, He Himself is most ready to be revealed. And if what we suffer draws us nearer to Him, we shall be content and shall be able, helped by Christ, to cry out, not in rebellion, but in faith.

"If we accept good from the hand of God, shall we not accept evil?"

———————— · ————————

The Paradox of Pain

Revelation 21.4 "Neither shall there be any more pain."

What terrific changes there have been in the past century — the motor car and the aeroplane; telephone and electricity;

radio and television; microchip, computer and video have revolutionised our lives. They are all wonderful, these inventions, but if I had to choose one which has done most to improve the quality of life for ordinary people, I would choose none of these but rather the discoveries of modern medicine — vaccination against smallpox, innoculation against the killing diseases of childhood and tuberculosis, X-rays, penicillin, cortisone and the rest. Tombstones in old churchyards tell their own story with their long lists of children who died in infancy or at a few years old in past generations, but it is not only in the prevention of early death that advances have been made. One of the greatest is in the relief of pain.

The fact that people in the past did not have all the mechanical and electrical gadgetry we have, did not, of itself, prevent them from living good and happy lives, but the unrelieved pain which many had to bear must have driven them to the very edge of despair and beyond. What women must have suffered in difficult childbirth before Sir James Y. Simpson began, in Edinburgh, to use chloroform to ease their pain! What agony old people with cancer or gangrene must have known! What soldiers wounded in battle must have endured is beyond imagining. And still many suffer, despite all the analgesics. The mystery of pain still confronts us.

Of course, there are some pains which are useful and which call attention to danger or disease. But beyond that which has any conceivable usefulness, there is an over-plus of pain which presents us with a problem and which has puzzled the best minds and the gentlest spirits throughout history. We might perhaps learn to bear our own pain with some kind of stoicism, but it is hard to watch the helpless distress of others — especially that of children or of the old. One cannot help but feel indignant when one hears the piteous cries of those who suffer. Why did a God of love for so long keep secret so many of the ways in which pain can be relieved? Why do so many still have so much to endure?

Certainly there are no professions more worthy of honour than those which are dedicated to the healing of disease and the relief of suffering. There is no duty more urgent than that of making available to people everywhere everything we know about how pain can be diminished. It is monstrous that in so many parts of the world, men and women and children are, at this moment, crying out in a pain which we have the means to relieve.

Jesus could never resist the appeal of human suffering. He saw pain as something alien and out of place in His Father's world. In the Book of Revelation in the 21st chapter, the great promises of God are piled one on top of the other — God will dwell with His people and be their God; He will wipe away all tears from their eyes; there will be no more death, neither sorrow nor crying. And then, almost as the pinnacle of the promises of God comes this — "Neither shall there be any more pain."

Yet, all that having been said, there is no doubt that people who have borne a great deal of pain seem, despite it — or as it sometimes appears, because of it — to have become better people. Some of the greatest music — Mozart's Clarinet Concertos for example, and some of the noblest poetry — Milton's Sonnet on his Blindness — have come out of pain.

What is true of the great is true also of ordinary folk. Those to whom we go when we are in distress are those who themselves have suffered. J. M. Barrie, speaking of the death of a child in his family, said that that was what gave his mother her soft eyes and drew all sufferers to her gentleness. Think of the very kindest person you know. Is it not someone who has suffered a great deal?

Has not God shown the way? Knowing no pain Himself, He has borne the pain of all. Isaiah saw this first. "He was wounded for our transgressions. He was bruised for our iniquities. The chastisement of our peace was upon Him and with His stripes we are healed."

That most profound and moving of prophecies found no fulfilment till a Man walked in Galilee, who felt the pain of every sufferer He met, who finally in the agony of the Crucifixion made Himself one with the agony of all mankind. Now we know that the greatest sufferer of all is God, not in and for Himself, but in and for all His children. That is why we dare not inflict, nor fail to relieve, distress. "Inasmuch", said Christ "as you have done it or done it not to one of the least of these my brethren, you have done it or done it not to me."

At this moment if anyone is hungry, Christ is hungry; if anyone is thirsty, Christ is thirsty; if anyone is sick or in prison, Christ is sick or in prison. It is Christ who has been maimed or bereaved in the Lebanon or in Ulster. It is Christ who feels needless pain in Africa, India or the Caribbean. Christ is in every stinking slum in the world where children are groomed for crime. Christ feels for the thousands of innocent unborn, some able to feel pain, who are destroyed every year in our own country.

Like as a father pitieth his children, so the Lord pitieth. At this moment God is looking at every man, woman and child in pain and is feeling for each what the best and kindest of fathers feels for his suffering child. If once we realise that that is so, we shall not rest till, at whatever sacrifice, the vast pain of the world's millions is relieved, and, in the meantime, all sufferers know that there is Another in it with them, One who has a right to speak out of the depths of His own agony and who has the power to help. For where pain is, there is Christ in His pity. When once we see that this is so, the desperate tides of the whole world's anguish will no longer ebb and flow unheeded by us in our pampered security. However free of pain we may meantime be ourselves, we shall learn gentleness and compassion for those in any part of God's world who are in pain, and we will do more — far more — than we have been doing to hasten the day when Christ shall suffer no more the pain of His children, when His perfect will shall be done on earth as it is in Heaven — and there shall be no more pain.

---·---

What is the Matter, Hagar?
(A study of self-pity)

Genesis 21.17 "What is the matter, Hagar?"

At first sight this is a very silly question. "What is the matter, Hagar?" It was perfectly obvious what was wrong with Hagar. She was hungry and thirsty and homeless and her son was about to die. "What is the matter, Hagar?" indeed!

You remember the story. When Sarah had no children, Hagar bore Abraham a son, Ishmael — said to be Mohammed's ancestor. Hagar, quite sure that Sarah would never have children, jeered at her. Beyond any expectation, Sarah in her old age gave birth to Isaac. As soon as he was born, Sarah, always a little jealous of Hagar and Ishmael, grew more and more so. One of the saddest things about sin is that it infects our best and purest emotions. At any rate, Sarah's hatred grew like a malignant cancer of the soul, till she could no longer stand the sight of Hagar and her boy. The Chinese sign for Peace is a little house with one woman in it. The Chinese sign for War is a little house with two women in it! So Sarah went to work on Abraham. "Drive out this slave-girl and her son; I will not have this slave-girl's son sharing the inheritance with my son Isaac." The authentic sound of the stairhead row is here. Hagar is not named. She becomes "this slave-girl". Abraham, poor man, loved both his boys, Ishmael and Isaac, and could not see why Sarah could not too. But Sarah could not, and would nag him from dawn to dusk. So finally, for peace's sake — and what frightful things we do for peace — Abraham sent Hagar and Ishmael away.

This is not quite so bad as it sounds. They were wandering Bedouins these. With any luck, Hagar would find a protector among another tribe and do not too badly. But she had no luck. At last she and the boy were on the point of death. She put the child under a bush and she herself went off so as not to see him die.

It was at this point that God asked her, "What is the matter, Hagar?" Well, she could have told Him. From a position of honour, she had become a wandering beggar. Her son, at one time heir presumptive to Abraham, had become a pauper. Now they were both likely to die. Hagar knew what was wrong all right, and whose fault — God's, Who had not led her to an oasis or a friendly tribe; Abraham's, for being so weak; Sarah's, who in her own happiness and good fortunes had been pitiless. If Hagar put up any such argument, God would ask again, "What is the matter, Hagar?" Not "What's the matter with the world, or God, or Abraham or Sarah", but "What is the matter with you?"

Underlying all Hagar's troubles was one single cause. The hunger, the thirst, the loneliness, the loss, all seemed separate troubles, but they all arose from the one fact — that she had been sent away by Abraham. That arose from Sarah's insistent demand that she should be; and that in turn arose from her own attitude in the days when Sarah was childless.

When we land in trouble, we are apt to see a whole range of causes. But if we trace back, all arise from one cause. We stay up too late watching some silly programme on television, so we lie abed next morning and blame our wives. We burn our mouths with too hot tea or coffee. We run for our train and miss it. We argue with the station manager that it went before its time. Before the day ends, we've fallen out all round and feel that everybody is a fool or a rogue or both. In point of fact, none of these things would have happened if we had gone to bed at a decent time. There was only one cause for our bad day and that cause was ourselves.

"The fault, dear Brutus, is not in our stars but in ourselves." Once we stop blaming the stars, we can set about putting things right. So long as we are obsessed with other people's faults and failures, we shall wallow in despair and self-pity. We shall rouse ourselves to deal with our miseries or misfortunes only when we accept our share of responsibility for them, when we face the question, "What is the matter?"

The Authorised Version makes it clear that this question implies one underlying cause of all Hagar's troubles, and that cause is within herself — "What ails *thee*, Hagar?" The cure of course, therefore, is to be sought nowhere else than in Hagar's own mind and will and heart. God did not send her a parcel of food or a bottle of water or money or a husband. He aroused new courage and new hope within her and a new and less sentimental love of her son. "Get to your feet, lift the child up and hold him in your arms." And God opened her eyes and she saw a well of water. It had been there all the time. She had been so sorry for herself that she hadn't looked.

It is so easy and so tempting to blame our troubles on other people, or on ill health, or on our environment, or on our bad luck. No doubt none of these is perfect. But God can do nothing with us until we stop excusing ourselves and blaming others, until we begin to excuse others and to blame ourselves. For it is only when we admit our own responsibility that God can speak His healing word of pardon and start us off afresh to do the best that we can with what of life remains.

That is the forgiveness of sins, and it all begins with an honest answer to the question, "What ails thee?" The real trouble with me is me. Don't look behind you, nor to the right, nor to the left. Look into the eyes of Christ and look within you. Take responsibility for your own faults and your own follies and your own sins, and then accept the forgiveness of God in Christ, and accept — as Hagar did — the chance of a new beginning.

"What is the matter, Hagar?" What ails *thee*? Once you know, listen to Christ. "Take heart, my son — my daughter —; your sins are forgiven." And start afresh with Him today.

HEALING

Jesus the Healer

Matthew 14.14 "Jesus — saw a great crowd; his heart went out to them, and he cured those of them that were sick."

Not many weeks pass without the problem of evil confronting us. Television presents us with pictures of massacres, civil wars, and mass starvation. Although not on such a huge scale, most ordinary lives are also touched by tragedy sooner or later. Sad, inexplicable things are constantly happening no farther away than some house in our own street, or even in our own homes.

If there were no God, there is, of course no problem. Whatever happens, happens — and that is that. We need not look for sense or meaning in a life which is simply a succession of accidents in a meaningless, materialistic universe. Those of us, however, who not only believe in God, but believe in a God of love, cannot help but torment ourselves with the attempt to square our faith in God's love with our experience of a life which seems so often to be cruel and senseless.

The Bible does not dodge the problem of evil. On the contrary, it thrusts every daunting, bewildering fact before us. Jesus Himself wrestled with it — the death of His friend Lazarus caused Him to weep; the fall of the tower of Siloam perplexed Him; the plight of sick folk, the terrible cries of the insane man on the Gadarene shore tore at His heart. All the problems we face, He faced, right up to His agony in Gethsemane and His own terrible death on Calvary. Make no mistake. He faced the problem of evil in its myriad forms more honestly than any other has or will, faced them with a heart sensitised by love, faced them and came through with His faith in the Father's love undimmed. How did He do it?

The answer is the three phrases of our text: He saw a great crowd. His heart went out to them. He cured those of them who were sick.

1. He saw a great crowd.

An Eastern crowd is not a pretty sight on a hot day, especially when those who make it up are jostling for position, carrying friends with every conceivable sort of disease. Your tendency and mine would be to look away. Not so Christ. He not only looked at them. He *saw* them. Do we see the unhappy victims of natural disasters or of their fellows' cruelty, who are so often on the television news? Do we really see them as people?

Once, in the house of Simon the Pharisee, a woman of bad reputation appeared, and Jesus asked Simon, "Do you see this woman?" If Simon had replied, he might have said, "I see her all right. I know her sort." But what Christ wanted to know was whether Simon saw the woman as a person, as a child of God. Like all sophisticated people, Simon had everybody sorted out into categories. We do the same. We listen to accents. We, ever so tactfully, enquire about school, the father's job, and so on. Then we decide whether they are "our sort" or not. All the time our eyes are skimming over the surface of people, classifying them. But we don't *see* them — not as people. Do we really see the unhappy people starving in Ethiopia, in Haiti, in Bangladesh? If we did, would we not do more for them? Do we really need caviare while they lack bread?

The first thing we must learn of Christ is how to see — see beyond the stoicism of the persecuted, see beyond the indifference or cynicism or bitterness of our neighbours to the wistful, weary, questing soul beneath. We must learn not just to admit that there is evil in the world, but to see with the eyes of Christ the pain and sorrow and bewilderment and despair of so many in distant lands and round about our own doors.

2. His heart went out to them.

But let us beware. For if we are led by Christ really to see other people, then we shall be led by Him to take the second step. When He saw the crowd, "His heart went out to them." How would we have reacted to the clamouring mass of human need? — in despair perhaps, or in irritation or in fury with the National Health Service or with the Department of Social Security? But Christ's sole reaction was of compassion. The word "compassion" means to suffer with. It applies in its completeness only to Christ who suffered with every sick or sad or sinning soul He met, and finally on Calvary suffered for us all. But in the measure and degree in which we have the spirit of Christ, we too will suffer with those about us.

"Be kind," said Ian McLaren, "for most folk are having a hard battle." If we see that that is so, we shall pity them until it hurts. The commandment, "Love your neighbour as yourself", is constantly misunderstood to mean, "Love your neighbour as much as you love yourself." That is nonsense. I cannot love myself. I may pamper myself or admire myself, but love demands another person. What the commandment means — and the late Professor Barclay agreed with me once that so it could be interpreted — is "You shall love your neighbour as one like yourself" — as a child of God with the same longings and needs, the same yearnings, the same dreams, the same shames and the same agonies as you yourself have — the same origin — the same destiny. If we see people so, we shall treat each person we meet with perfect seriousness and utter courtesy as a son or daughter of the most high God, a brother or sister for whom also Christ died.

And if we see with the eyes of Christ and feel with the heart of Christ, then inevitably we will be led on to the third step he took: Jesus saw a great crowd, *and* His heart went out to them, *and*

3. He cured those of them who were sick.

I suppose Jesus could have said, "There are millions of sick people in the world and tens of thousands in Palestine. Why should I bother with the few who happen to be near at hand? Should I not concentrate on preaching and teaching and not waste my time and soil my hands by touching blind eyes and withered limbs and leprous sores?" But He could not keep Himself out of people's troubles, or hold Himself back from doing what He could to help.

Nor should we. The fact that we cannot do everything in a world drenched with tears should not stop us doing what we can. So long as we see evil as a problem to be solved by our cleverness, a solution to it will become ever more elusive. When we see evil as a challenge to be met and try to meet it, we shall come to an understanding of the heart lying far deeper than our minds.

By and by all will be made plain. Of that I am certain. But it will not be in this world, and we should be content to wait till on the other side much that is now mysterious will at last be made clear. So long as we see evil as an intellectual problem to be solved, we shall remain coldly locked up in our intellectual pride. It is only when we see evil as a summons to action, as opportunity for service, a challenge to do something, however little, about it, that we shall begin to suffer with Christ and with our fellows, and begin to understand and to pity. The Cross means that finally God suffers with us, suffers with us that we may suffer with and succour our fellows in humble imitation of Him who

> saw a great crowd, and
> whose heart went out to them, and who
> cured those of them who were sick.

—————— · ——————

His Hands

Luke 4.40 "He laid his hands on them one by one, and cured them."

John 20.20 "He showed them his hands."

Luke 24.50 "He blessed them with uplifted hands."

Anyone who has seen Albrecht Dürer's famous picture "Praying Hands" can never afterwards think of hands as unimportant. The point of the painting, of course, is that the hands are not lily white, but are scarred, stained and gnarled — the hands of one who has worked and suffered. A moment's thought will confirm Dürer's suggestion of the vast significance of hands. Often they indicate the owner's calling or occupation. There are the large and sinewy hands of the blacksmith; the tapering, sensitive fingers of the artist; the thickened and muscular, and wonderfully skilful hands of the fisherman; the strong but gentle hands of the surgeon; the work-worn, beloved hands of the mother. What a picture is conjured by the description "Deft and sure, there was no hurry in her hands."

Faces deceive almost as often as they reveal, but not hands. Watch that calm and placid face! Only the hands clasping and unclasping or tightly clenched show the inner conflict, the unquiet mind, the carefully controlled anger. How cruel hands can be, and how kind; how grasping and greedy; how friendly and generous!

How wonderful Our Lord's hands must have been! They were not clean and soft like a preacher's, but useful looking and yet gentle too. They must have been skilled hands that could wield a chisel or an axe and reef a sail, or help to haul a net in time of need. They were not too fine to touch leprous sores and fevered brows, and eyes with the frightful, repulsive crusts so often seen in the East. In the Gospel of Luke we read that, "At sunset all who had friends suffering from one disease or another brought them to him; and he laid his hands on them one by one and cured them."

In the days to come, if our hands are reluctant to turn to the necessary, humble tasks of life — to washing or writing, to cleaning or healing, cooking or serving, let us look at them and remember those other hands. They did not rebel at the routine tasks of the carpenter's shop, or shrink from the most loathsome contacts, and even at the end were found washing the disciples' feet. "He laid his hands on them one by one and cured them."

But there was one disease so virulent and deep-seated that even Christ's hands could not heal it, one hurt so fearful it could only be cured by His own suffering. Disease of the body fled before Him, but the disease of the human heart, sin, seems only to have grown more malignant. Resistant to the pathos of the Last Supper and the agony of the Garden, men seemed unmoved at the majestic compassion of the Cross. Still unhealed, they looked on, and when the first news came of His rising, there were some even of His disciples sceptical and suspicious. So He made the supreme appeal which St John records. The disciples were huddled together behind closed doors of fear. To them came Christ. "Peace be with you!" He said, and then showed them His hands and His side. So when the disciples saw the Lord, "they were filled with joy" — joy, for here was the proof of the love of God and proof of the power of God — the nailprints in the hands of the Risen Son of God.

If, when we feel our lot is hard and our sufferings greater than we deserve; if, when our hands clench in rebellion, or are clasped in desperate anxiety, we could visualise two hands in which are nailprints, our querulous complaining would melt into wondering gratitude and adoring praise, "He showed them his hands."

When finally Christ left the disciples to face the immense task of spreading His Gospel to the uttermost parts of the earth; left them with so many questions still unanswered, with only the promise of persecution and an almost certain martyrdom, the last they saw of Him was with His hands raised in blessing. St Luke tells us in the few last verses of his Gospel that Christ led His disciples out as far as Bethany, and "He blessed them with uplifted hands."

So, if at times the burden of our work for the Gospel seems too heavy, or our frustration too grievous; if at times the Kingdom seems to be coming so slowly as hardly to be said to be coming at all; if we feel the need for greater certainty, more assurance than we have, then surely the Lord, if we ask Him, will lead us out towards the peace of some Bethany, and, lifting up His hands, will bless us too. And there will be peace in our souls again and power in our lives, and a deathless hope in our hearts.

"He laid his hands on them one by one, and cured them." "He showed them his hands." "He blessed them with uplifted hands."

And those hands so quick to heal, so ready to suffer, so sure to bless, are the hands into which we may surely commit ourselves and our dear ones, certain that they are still the same, and always will be. If, in helplessness or fierce temptation, in heart-break or weariness or despair, we lift our hands in prayer, quite surely they will be met and held by His.

And when at length, with darkened eyes and fingers cold, we seek some last, loved hand to hold — ready, eager to help and comfort and receive us on the other side will be — His hands.

An Embarrassing Interruption
(Bartimaeus and us)

Mark 10.51 "Jesus said, 'What do you want me to do for you?'"

Jericho, a miserable little town, was probably rather pleased with the excitement of Jesus' visit. He was making an almost royal progress through the town, when the whole thing was spoiled by the raucous bawling of this blind beggar at the roadside. People tried to shut him up, but he refused to be silent. It was just one of those unfortunate, embarrassing interruptions that spoil great occasions.

Our Lord was on the way to Jerusalem, with Gethsemane, the trial and Calvary before Him, the whole fate of the Jewish people in the balance, the destiny of mankind being worked out. In the middle of the majestic drama, a blind beggar's shouts. For anyone else this would have been an intolerable interruption, a nuisance, a distraction, an anti-climax — but not for Jesus. With perfect courtesy, with the air of unhurried patience He always had, Jesus called the man out. With the salvation of the world weighing on His heart, He stood still and waited for a blind beggar. Throwing aside his beggar's cloak, sure that he would never need it again, Bartimaeus moved forward — and then, "What do you want me to do for you?" Extraordinary! Surely it was obvious! Yet Jesus never wasted words. Why did He ask this?

By the question, Jesus excluded the crowds, the disciples, everybody else but the beggar and Himself. "What do *you* want?" — let the man speak for himself. He has a request. Let him make it. No-one but Christ has ever had the same ability to take each person by himself or herself and give each His whole attention. Half the time when we are speaking to someone, we're literally or metaphorically looking over their shoulder to see who else more interesting is coming; or else we're talking so loudly that we don't hear what they say; or we're too busy classifying them or judging them. But not Jesus.

For these few moments, there were only Bartimaeus and Himself in the world.

So it is always. Jesus does not look upon us as a statistic or a unit or a vague faceless thing. To Him we are, each of us, individuals. To each He says, "What do *you* want me to do for you?" — and then He waits for our answer. From each He will receive a different answer. In any group of people, not two will be alike. One will have a new joy, one a new fear, one a vast relief, one a sorrow. We each have our thing — loneliness, sickness, fear of age, moral defeat. Never a church service goes by but Christ halts before each one of us and asks "And you? What do you want me to do for you?"

Note who is asking the question, "'What do you want *me* to do for you?" Of anyone else, Bartimaeus would have asked for money or food, but not from Christ. He scaled up his demands to correspond to the greatness of the Questioner. This was what called forth Christ's power. Here was a man ready to ask enough. Of course, Christ is interested in our desires, however trivial. "Give us this day our daily bread." But what constantly bewildered and disappointed Christ was how little people expected of Him. "If you have faith no bigger than a mustard-seed, you will say to this mountain, 'Move from here to there!' and it will move; nothing will prove impossible for you."

There are people who say, "let's be realistic." Very well, let's be realistic. We have the power of Almighty God to draw upon. Infinite resources are ours.

"Thou art coming to a King.

Large petitions thou must bring."

Somehow, our requests must match His great-heartedness. "What do you want *me* to do for you?"

Last of all, notice that Christ is willing and eager to do things for us. "What do *you* want *me* to *do for you?*" All the time, we are apt to think of what we can do for Him. Goodness knows, there's plenty to be done in our country and in the world. But the first question Jesus asks is always, "What do you want me to do?" Bartimaeus followed Christ, we are told, and no doubt he gave of his best to Christ's service, but first he was given his sight. What a wonderful thing it must have been that the first face he would look on would be the face of Christ. Perhaps what most of us need above all others is to have our eyes opened, that we may see Christ. Amidst all the dreadful clouds and fearful darkness of our world, if we could only see Christ clearly, all the rest would make sense — all the other pieces of the jig-saw of our lives would fall into place. Perhaps, rather than make any other request, we — each of us — should ask just this, "Master, I want my sight."

But we must mean it. Sometimes nobody would be more surprised than we if our prayers were answered. We ask to be delivered from this sin or that, but we don't really expect it to happen — don't really *want* it to happen. Let's tell the truth in our prayers. It's no use asking for what we don't want. If you are conscious of a real need, such as you can ask for in the name of Christ, then, in God's name, it can be met. It may not be as we ask it, nor when we ask it, but in God's good time and in God's own way. Always He answers our prayers, even if only to give us of Himself. And if once we have Christ, there is not much else we need, but daily bread for daily need till journey's end, and then the assurance of a welcome home.

There it is then, in all its profound simplicity. Jesus of Nazareth is passing by, as surely as on the Jericho Road — is passing by quite near. There's a stillness. He's by your side. Listen to what He says — and He means it, every word of it.

"What do you want me to do for you?"
"Master, I want my sight."

The Hem of His Garment
(The value of an incomplete faith)

Mark 5.28 (NEB) "If I touch even his clothes, I shall be cured."

No story of healing in the New Testament bears more clearly the marks of authenticity. Not only must this type of ailment have been very hard to cure before surgery was much used, but it is typical that the patient in her distress would go from doctor to doctor, sometimes seeming to be a little better and sometimes a little worse. Now she was at the end of her tether and at the end of her money. She would not want to tell Our Lord her symptoms in front of a whole crowd of people, but despair drove her on. "Perhaps if I can touch him," she thought to herself," even touch the hem of his garment, I'll be healed."

On the face of it, of course, it was sheer superstition, the belief that there was some magic power in the clothes of Jesus, a kind of fetishism. And yet, of course, it worked. Somehow Jesus felt the woman's nearness and her need and met it, and in the moment of meeting it, knew Himself that virtue had gone out of Him.

There is such a thing as spiritual or psychological or physical energy which can be tapped by other people, and of which one can be drained. Let me give you a simple personal illustration. Two weeks ago, I played 18 holes of very bad but very energetic golf. Later on in the day I was ready for a good walk. One week ago, I spent two and a half hours with sick people and was utterly exhausted. So Jesus, feeling the desperation of this woman's need and her confidence that He could help, let His healing compassion flow out to her, despite the very rudimentary nature of her faith.

There is much comfort for us all, in that Christ does not demand complete comprehension nor even true faith, just so long as there is a genuinely felt need and an honest confidence in Him. He will respond to the most ignorant, imperfect and feeble faith, if only it be genuine. There are many on the periphery of the Church, or even outside of it altogether, who none the less know their need and know deep down that it can be met in Christ.

I once knew two dear old ladies, both long since dead, who lived in one of the slummier parts of Glasgow. They never missed church, morning and evening, but hardly any of their neighbours ever came. One of these neighbours, a woman of very disorderly life, met my two old ladies one Sunday coming from church. Putting out a hand she said, "You've been to church. Let me touch you and maybe I'll get a wee share of the blessing too." Gross superstition or real but imperfect faith? I think Christ would have given her the benefit of the doubt.

In Mexico and in some parts of Quebec and France, I have marvelled at the materialistic forms of Christianity — the flickering candles, the little bunches of flowers, the crude stucco statuettes, the fragments of wood said to be of Christ's Cross, being venerated, and the scraps of lace, said to be of Mary's veil, and the relics of the saints. All nonsense of course. Mistaken and misdirected — and yet, and yet. There is something real behind it all. One has only to sense the intensity of devotion of these simple worshippers, to be ashamed of one's own cold faith. May it not be that these folk, kneeling before their relics have a deeper sense of need and a simpler trust in God, than we who read books about Him?

I recently read an account of a pilgrimage in Peru. The writer tells of all sorts of strange and ignorant beliefs, haunting by the restless spirits of those who have committed a mortal sin, and so on. The pilgrimage ends at a rock bearing the image of Christ before which hundreds of the pilgrims cry and pray. The author asked "Why do they cry?" and got the answer, "They cry for the sufferings of El Senor, the Lord." Can we, who have never shed a tear for Christ, despise their devotion?

Is our own faith, at any rate, perfect and complete? Not many of us have a face to face and heart to heart relationship with Jesus. Some of the saints may know him well but the most that the rest of us can hope for is some kind of indirect knowledge of Him. The Sacrament is such. Bread is bread, and bread it remains, and wine is wine. The same is true of the Church, of the Bible and much else. In these we do not come face to face with Christ. Rather, coming near Him, we touch the hem of his garment.

When Sir James Simpson, who first used chloroform as an anaesthetic, was dying, a friend said that soon, like the beloved disciple John, he would be leaning on Jesus' breast. Sir James replied, "I don't know that I can quite do that, but I think I have got hold of the hem of His garment." Would any of us, could any of us claim more?

And it is a comfort to know that, even if we have no very clearly formulated religious convictions, no real grasp of the Christian faith, no right to an inner place in the circle round about Christ. Even so, if we have a knowledge of our need, if we have a strong feeling that Christ can help as no other can, then He will. The most hesitant belief that Christ is the Saviour of the world and my Saviour will be enough for Him at first. We shall receive according to our faith, and on the most slender of foundations Christ will build.

"If I touch even his clothes, I shall be cured."

There is one thing more, and that is a strange thing. Feeling herself healed, the woman would quite happily have slipped away without being noticed. Why did Christ not allow her to do so? Was it not cruel of Him to call this poor woman, diffident and ashamed, out of the crowd to acknowledge what she had done? Why did He do it? Consider what would have happened if He had not done so. The woman would have gone home without having met Christ, but talking of what power there was in His clothes. She would have believed and led others to believe that healing lay in the fringes of His garment and not in the compassion of His heart. By calling her out, Jesus established the personal relationship with her in which faith consists. The touch on the hem of His garment may have healed her disease; the conversation with Christ made her whole. It was not her finger but her faith that healed her and it was not the hem of His garment but the love of Christ that is the cause of our salvation.

It may be that you and I are delivered from the depth of our despair by touching the garments of Christ — the Church, the Sacraments, the Bible. But only if these things lead us to Christ Himself, will we find peace of mind.

"Give me of Thyself", prayed St Augustine, "without which, though thou shouldest give me all else the world contains, yet cannot I be satisfied."

If we but touch the hem of Christ's garment, it is much, and we shall find healing and help. But only if, in response to His invitation, we stand before Him, hesitant and ashamed it may be, but ready to receive His grace, shall we find the fulness of life which is His will for us all.

The End of Tears
(and their value in this life)

Revelation 21.4 (AV) "God shall wipe away all tears from their eyes."

A good case can be made out for the assertion that the 21st chapter of Revelation is the most wonderful thing in the world — far surpassing any work of art, any invention of man, or anything else that has ever been written. It is impossible to assess the comfort and strength brought through the centuries to billions of the sad, the enslaved, and the persecuted by the promise it contains. Possibly the greatest verse in the chapter is this: "God shall wipe away all tears from their eyes."

Think of the rivers of tears that have flowed from the beginning of time until now. Think of the tears — the bitter,

bitter tears — that flowed in two world wars. Think of the tens of thousands of hungry children in so many lands, crying with hunger at this moment, the tears of helpless invalids, of the abandoned wife, of the mother or father whose child has gone wrong — tears of sorrow, tears of shame, tears of self-pity, tears of helplessness, tears of compassion. The great God who has made all things heeds them all. He does not despise our tears, or tell us briskly to be done with them. Instead, He promises that one day He will wipe them away with His own hand. I believe that, for is He not like Christ, who could not see pain without stretching out His hand to help, who had compassion on the multitude?

Yet, of course, the more clearly we see the picture and accept the promise, as I do, that there will be an end of pain and sorrow and tears, the more bewildering the question becomes. "Why tears at all?" If God is so loving and compassionate, why does He permit His children to suffer as they do? When He was fashioning the world, surely He could have fashioned it in such a way that no tears would ever need to have been shed. Why does He allow the things to happen in the world which cause tears? Read any newspaper, sit in any court of law, walk through the wards of any hospital, and the question rises up to hit you. "Why could God not order things otherwise, so that life would be pleasant all the time?"

Certainly, there are many areas in life so dark and fearful that it is impossible to see why a God of love permits them — malformed babies, cancer, senile dementia — the light of the Gospel hardly seems to touch these. For the explanation of why a God of love permits such things, we must reverently wait till we are told on the other side. Meantime we can but pray for the means to be found to avoid or alleviate some of these fearful conditions.

Yet, would we really and truly want a life entirely without tears? If we were offered on the one hand life as it is with all its perplexities, sorrows and pain, and on the other a life in which we would feel nothing, which would we choose? It is not a question to be too casually or quickly answered. I think I would take life as it is. In my congregation many years ago, a young man was killed in an accident at his work, leaving a widow and child. No doubt in pity, the doctor gave the poor young woman a supply of tablets. When I arrived to take the funeral, she was hilarious, laughing at anything and nothing. No tears I have ever seen were so terrible as was that laughter.

Aldous Huxley's *Brave New World* depicts a life without sorrow or pain. One of the citizens does not like it and says, "I don't want comfort. I want God. I want poetry. I want danger. I want freedom." Aghast, the Controller says, "But you'll be very unhappy." "Well," said the other, "I claim the right to be unhappy." Would we not all claim the same right, rather than accept, in place of life as we know it, a mush of superficial pleasure? I knew an old lady who, after her husband's death, lived in a great house, alone with her memories. She used to say, "I have learned to let neither joy nor sorrow affect me." Surely most of us would pity rather than envy her. We have a right to our tears.

But, if that be true, what are we to make of the promise in our text? If at last, God wipes all tears from our eyes, if in heaven there is no more pain or sorrow, will life there not be as bland and shallow and savourless as a tearless life here could be? If God wipes away all tears, will He not also wipe away all love and depth and majesty and glory from life?

It might seem so, but the eyes that have wept are never the same again. The heart which has suffered will be gentler for it. Those whose tears have dried are not the same as those who have never wept. The memory of the tears remains. Those who have passed through the glen of weeping emerge as better, kinder, braver folk than they were before. J. M. Barrie, telling of the death of a child in his family, says that the sorrow is what gave his mother her soft eyes and drew all sufferers to her gentleness. Sorrow was its meaning and purpose. God gave us tears to weep. When they have done their work with us, He wipes them all away, but the remembrance of them will never fade.

I have no pat answer to the problems of evil and pain and sorrow. Any answer I could give would be unworthy of the dignity of tears and the agony of pain. I can say and do say that there will be an end. The day will come when there will be no more death, neither sorrow nor crying, neither shall there be any more pain. Meantime God is in the thing with us. Is that not enough? He sympathises with us in our grief, for He knows the feel of a broken heart and the bitterness of weeping. The hand that wipes our tears has nail-prints in it.

——————— · ———————

THE CHRISTIAN LIFE

Have You Been Saved?
(The value of endurance)

Matthew 10.22 (RSV) "He who endures to the end will be saved".

Earnest people periodically buttonhole one and ask, "Have you been saved?" It is an important question — possibly finally the only important question, but it is a hard question to answer. Is salvation an instantaneous thing which is perfect and complete in a moment of time? In a sense, yes. The thing happened when from Calvary Hill there echoed the great cry, "It is finished." I was saved at the moment when Christ died for our sins, and not for our sins only, but for the sins of the world. I am part of the world Jesus came to save. I claim my share in the salvation he wrought.

Yet those earnest people who ask, "Have you been saved?" don't want an answer in terms of what Christ once accomplished. They want to know if something very decisive happened at one point in your life. Let it be said that it is thus that some of the greatest saints started out on the Christian Way after a sudden conversion. To Paul it came in the blinding light which struck him down on the Damascus road. To Luther it came twice: once when he was caught in a terrible thunderstorm, and once later when he was climbing the penitential stairway in Rome. To C. S. Lewis it came in the course of a journey: when it began he was an atheist; when it ended he was a Christian. But this is not how it happens to all of us, and it need not happen so. And even when it does happen, it is not the end of the matter, but only the beginning — and these saints would be the first to acknowledge that.

So to my inquisitive friend's question, "Have you been

207

saved?", I would be bound to answer, "Not yet, but I hope and believe I'm on the way. It is not complete, but at least I'm in process of being saved." For to be saved means not to be saved from the penalty of sin, but being saved — being delivered, from sin itself. And daily I hope it is happening. To believe otherwise would be to doubt the grace of God. The thing has begun, I really believe. It began at my baptism, as it will begin for every baby baptised. But though it began for me so long ago, it is very far from being complete. There are large areas of my life where self-seeking and prejudice and vanity still hold sway — grace resistant areas. The Bible accepts the gradualness of salvation. It knows nothing of perfect salvation, brought about in a moment and lasting for ever. It speaks rather of patient continuance in well-doing. "Continue in the faith", said Paul. And three times over in the words of the text, Jesus himself said, "He that endures to the end will be saved."

It is the enduring that counts — not the beginning. The French have a saying, "It's the first step that counts". But they are wrong. Well begun may be important, but it's not everything. It's not the first step, but the last that wins the race. I can run as fast as Sebastian Coe any day — for one pace. I can play a Bach prelude on the organ — at least the first note. I can climb Mount Everest — at least the first yard of it. But it's not the first pace, the first note, the first yard that matters. It's not the beginning. It's the keeping going that counts. To quote Sir Francis Drake, a great sailor and a good man, on the day he sailed into Cadiz in 1587,

"O, Lord God, when Thou givest to Thy servants to endeavour any great matter, grant us to know that it is not the beginning but the continuing of the same until it be thoroughly finished which yieldeth the true glory, through Him that, for the finishing of Thy work, laid down His life, Our Redeemer, Jesus Christ."

It's the keeping going that counts.

I married a lovely young girl recently to a fine young man. It was a wonderful wedding and a joyous experience for me to have a share in it. But even more wonderful was a visit I paid earlier in the week to an old, old couple. The husband is totally blind now. When I was in, he put out his hand to try to find something on the table. His wife gently guided the hand and he smiled and said, "Thank you, my dear." That is what marriage means — not just the ceremony, not just the rapture. It's not the beginning that counts — not by itself. It's beginning well and keeping going to the end.

"He that endures to the end shall be saved." To the end! "There is no discharge in this warfare." So said Ecclesiastes, and Kipling took it up:

"Foot, foot, foot, foot, slogggin' over Africa,
Boots, boots, boots, boots, movin' up and down again.
There is no discharge in the war."

In the same vein, Christina Rossetti wrote:

"Does the road wind uphill *all* the way?"
'Yes, to the very end.'
"Will the day's journey take the *whole* long day?"
'From morn to night, my friend.'

He that endures *to the end* shall be saved.

But how? We all have our spells of weariness — of boredom in our work, of irritation with our families. The same is true of our religion. At times it doesn't seem to be getting anywhere. We're no better, nor greatly worse. Prayers seem pointless and services tedious and repetitious. Our little stock of faith forever runs away like sand through our fingers. The vision fades. Our love grows cold. Our goodness is as the morning cloud. Our last good resolutions join the heap of others in the scrapyard of the will — full of broken vows, purposes of good which came to nothing, high endeavours which petered out in failure and cynical disillusionment.

If none shall be saved except those who endure to the end, what hope have we? Should we flog our weary wills and try

again where we have so often failed? Yes, to some extent that
is the way. The perseverance of the saints is made up of an
infinite series of new beginnings.

But there's a better way — the way Isaiah knew.

"They who wait for the Lord shall renew their strength."

"They shall mount up with wings like eagles" — that's youth.

"They shall run and not be weary" — that's middle life.

And most blessed of all, "They shall walk and not faint."

Not in our own strength of purpose, not by the flogging of
our own weary will, shall we be saved, but by our humble
reliance upon the steadfast Love of God.

And nowhere else is that steadfast love so clearly shown as
in the life and death of Jesus, "the pioneer and perfecter of our
faith, who for the joy that was set before him endured the
cross, despising the shame". It is as we make Christ our pattern
and example, as we walk in His steps, that we shall be able
ourselves to endure to the end and by the mercy of God at last
be saved.

―――――― · ――――――

Do Something
(The need for action)

Acts 22.10 "What shall I do, Lord?"

This is the vital question. Till we ask it, we're just fooling
with religion. Once we've asked it, we've taken the first, crucial
step in Christian discipleship and there can be no turning
back. The reason why our Church is so flabby and ineffective
is because so many members are content to take an interest in
religion, but stop short of asking, "What can I do, Lord?"

It had taken Saul of Tarsus a long time to be ready to ask
this question. High-born, scholarly, strong-willed, he had
known all his life what he wanted to do. He knew he had a

great future. Quite sure of his own wisdom and his own righteousness, he was quick to defend his friend, the High Priest, and was foremost, therefore, in attacking the followers of Jesus the Galilean, whom the High Priest had condemned. When the Christians said that their dead Master was alive, Saul did not know whether to be amused or angry. The constancy of Stephen, the first martyr, may have dented his self-assurance a little, but that made him only the more determined to stamp the heresy out. If he had doubts, he thrust them down into his subconscious, but all the time he was learning more about this Christ, whom and whose followers he was persecuting.

Then suddenly on the Damascus Road he was stopped dead in his tracks and faced with this very Christ. Before he asked, he knew who it was. "Tell me, Lord, who you are." He knew that this was One whom even he, the proud, self-sufficient Saul, must address as Lord. "I am Jesus, whom you are persecuting", came the reply, and Paul knew that he had met his Master. It would never again be with him a case of doing what he wanted. With the simplicity and humility of a child, Saul — soon to be Paul — asked, "What shall I do, Lord?"

This is the crunch. This is the moment of truth, when the Will of God, revealed in Christ, displaces the will to power in the heart of men and women. It is a stage to which some of us never come. We believe in God — as Saul of Tarsus did — but we've no intention of letting Him rule our lives. All we want of Him is that He should help us to achieve our purposes. We say, not "What shall I do, Lord?", but "Lord, here is what you must do."

But God won't do what we tell Him to do. He will not be the servant of our desires, the instrument of our will to power. If we know what we want, let us go ahead and get it, but don't let us drag the Will of God into it. Once God comes in, our clamouring desires must be silent. *Our* plans, *our* purposes shrink before His majestic, wise and loving Will, and we can only ask, "What shall I do, Lord?"

Notice that Paul did not ask what his companions were to do, just what he himself should do; and this is the only question God will answer. Mark you, it is a lot pleasanter to think what other people should do, how they should behave. There is the story of the old black woman who cried, "Hallelujah! That's preaching!" as long as the Minister condemned the sins of the white folk. When he turned to dram drinking and snuff taking, which were her foibles, she said, "Tsch! Now he's quit preaching and started meddling." We love to hear everybody's sins denounced but ours, to learn about anybody's duty except our own. It's so much more fun to protest about the South Africans or the drug barons or the muggers of old ladies, than to confess one's own failures. But God never gossips. He'll never tell me what you or they should do, but only what I should do. Do you remember Peter asking about John? "Lord, what will happen to this man?" or, as the Authorised Version says, "Lord, what shall this man do?" And Christ's sharp reply, "What is it to you? Follow me." Still He's the same. The only question He'll answer is the one Saul asked, "What shall I do, Lord?"

Not what *I* want, but what *God* wants.

Not what God asks of somebody else, but His will for *me*.

Lastly, what God wants me to *do*.

It's no use chattering about God or to God, unless we are prepared — as of now — to do what He asks. There is only one possible answer to a lawful command in the Royal Navy. It is "Aye, Aye, Sir" — and it's the only answer to the command of God. God is not prepared to have a discussion with us about His purposes. He is prepared to tell us what to do and, if we do it, we shall be told all we need to know. There's a terrible psychological block which leads us to talk about Christ and to sing about Christ and to do nothing. Conviction that is not followed by action grows sour; which is part of the reason why the collection follows the preaching of the Word, that we may respond by our gifts to the proclamation of the generous love of God, that we may do *something*. Somehow the dreary sequence of conviction, resolution, no action — conviction, resolution, no action, must be broken. The log jam of the clogged will must be dynamited by our doing something.

"The native hue of resolution is sicklied o'er with the pale cast of thought, and enterprises of great pith and moment with this regard their currents turn awry, and lose the name of action." The great thing is to get things moving.

You know how it is. "I'm going to wash the car." "I should wash the car." "I'll maybe wash the car — tomorrow." And it is dirty still. "I'll write a cheque today." "I'll write a cheque soon." "I'll may be write a cheque." Your bank balance need not worry until the signature is written. It is the leap between thinking of doing something, wanting to do something, meaning to do something, and actually doing it which is hard to make.

So, if you are really ashamed of the way you've been fooling yourself by trying to fool God, *do* some one thing today. Start saying Grace before your lunch TODAY. Write that letter THIS AFTERNOON. Start praying again TONIGHT. Make the gift — TODAY, before the first passing sleeve rubs your resolution off before it has had a chance to dry and grow firm. Make a beginning in obedience to God and make it today. These things may seem tiny and remote from the race problem, crime, abortion, Ulster, inflation, drugs. But if you make a beginning with God, he will make a beginning with you out of all proportion to anything you've done.

Your life, your family, your Church, your nation will not be changed in a trice, but they'll *begin* to be. There will be a bridgehead in your life — maybe a tiny bridgehead, but that does not matter if it is a bridgehead for God. It was in a single human Life that the whole Grace of God was made free to the world. It was by the preaching of the Cross that the power of God was released. If the conviction of God's Grace in Christ has broken in on your soul, and the knowledge of your own condition and the need to make a change, then ask the same question as Paul did, and with the same seriousness, "What shall I do, Lord?" — and then, by the Grace of God, go and do it.

———————— · ————————

The Field of Lentils
(Struggling on in an uninspiring place)

2 Samuel 23.11-12 (paraphrase) "Shammah — stood his ground in a field of lentils and saved it and defeated the Philistines. So the Lord brought about a great victory."

Shammah was one of the three chief among David's thirty mighty men — the other two were Adino the Eznite and Eleazer. It was these three who went down later to Bethlehem, through the enemy lines, to fetch David a drink of water from his favourite well. But before telling us that great story, the writer of Samuel gives us a sample of the valour and strength of the three champions — three stories typical, no doubt, of many told about them.

Adino the Eznite slew 800 Philistines at one time with his spear; the second, Eleazer, defied the Philistines and fought on till the sword stuck in his hand. (The same was told of a Scottish sergeant at Waterloo where the blacksmith had to break the sword from its grip.)

The third, Shammah, stood in the midst of a piece of ground full of lentils and defended it. What a come down it might seem! What an anti-climax! There was no great distinction for Shammah here. Eleazer had fought with the Philistines gathered together for battle. Adino had slain 800 at once. Shammah won his victory, not amidst the shouts of champions but in a field of lentils; not with the sound of trumpets in his ears, but standing alone, cheered on by some old crofters and their womenfolk — uninspiring circumstances in which to fight.

The story is easy to reconstruct. Israel was in retreat. The Philistines were running rings round them. These lentils were a pretty vital source of food — high in protein. They grew about 18 inches high. The pod had only two peas in it. They were used for making a kind of red pease meal — Mujidderah — the same stuff which Esau sold in exchange for his birthright. It was used instead of wheat for bread by the poor or in time of scarcity. On the day in question, the farmer and his family were out to harvest the lentils. The Philistines were ready to swoop down to steal the crop, much as the Highlanders used to swoop down on the fertile Lowlands and disappear with corn and cattle. It had probably happened a dozen times before. The Philistine sergeant no doubt told his section that it was a piece of cake, or the Philistine equivalent to that. A small farmer ruined, a few families made hungry, one or two of the slow ones killed or wounded — a mere foraging skirmish with only a handful involved. It was to prevent this that Shammah fought. He stood in a field of lentils and defended it.

There was no thrill in it, no glory. Poor Shammah would hardly dare tell about it on winter nights round the barrack room fire. If he'd said "I won a victory in a field of lentils", one can imagine the guffaw which would have greeted him.

And yet, you know, probably most victories for God are won in a field full of lentils. In a town like this town, when someone says "No" when tempted to say "Yes"; in a family like your family, when someone is first to speak after a quarrel; in any house when a weary woman rises to look after a querulous invalid or a sick child; wherever and whenever men and women are doing battle, on however small a scale, with pride or greed or selfishness or dishonesty, why, it is there and then that the troop of the Philistines halt abashed and a feeble cheer rises from the throats of the few.

The ever growing menaces of drug addiction and obscenity and infidelity will not be halted by mighty movements. They will be halted when a tired man turns out to run a Scout troop or a Youth Club, or where a woman on top of a week's work takes a Sunday School class. It is these who, like Shammah, fight in the uninspiring surroundings of a field of lentils, who deserve a medal for valour.

For, of course, a field of lentils is not only an uninspiring place in which to do battle, it is also a very difficult place. To take up a prepared position on a river bank or on top of a hill is one thing, but to fight on a level plain is another, and the field of lentils would be flat. Anybody could have told Shammah that a field of lentils was no place to fight on — far better to let the Philistines have the crop, save his strength and wait until he had the advantage of them.

To all of that Shammah no doubt replied, "I know this is a poor position, but this is where God has placed me. The enemy is yonder and the food of these poor folk is at risk. So here I must stand and fight and trust God to win the victory." God did! When Luther faced the whole might and prestige of the Roman Catholic Church ranged against him, he said, "Here stand I. So help me God, I can do no other." So felt stout Shammah and in this uninspiring place he fought and God won for him the victory.

We all have our dreams of how well we could have done if our lot had been different. But, placed as we are, with routine tasks of no importance sapping our strength, how can we win? It is hard. Of course it is. But if it has to be done, it can be done, not in our own strength but in the strength of the Almighty God who has placed us where we are and who has called on us to make a stand and fight for it. Our field of lentils may hardly seem worth defending at times — uninspiring, difficult, but here God has placed us and here we must fight.

An uninspiring place, a difficult place and — an unexpected place.

A great deal of Shammah's victory was due to the element of surprise. The band of Philistines must have got quite a shock when, from a handful of fleeing farmers, a soldier emerged and stood his ground. They had grown used to jeering as the farmfolk ran. It may be, they thought that this was an ambush, some new stratagem. So there was — for, as the text says, the Lord came to help Shammah.

God loves to use surprise. Whenever He sees some Shammah make a stand, it is His delight to make sure that he wins.

When God came to the world, it was to an obscure corner of an obscure land, to live in a joiner's back shop. Not at all where *we'd* have expected the Son of God to live. Not the most inspiring place, nor the easiest from which to set out to conquer the world.

And when the last decisive battle was fought, that was in an uninspiring place enough, a quite unexpected place and one cruelly hard for Christ, for it was on a Cross.

It is by the Cross our victory will be won, if only we will cease our shameful flight and make a stand against the Devil. It is in the Cross that we shall find inspiration to be like Shammah who stood his ground in a field of lentils and defended it — and the Lord won a great victory.

So tomorrow it will be, for most of you, back to the factory or the store, to the office, the hospital, the school or the kitchen. It's not much fun at times. It's hard to keep going and to keep faithful. But where we are is where God has set for us to stand in our particular field of lentils and defend it. If we do, the Lord will win a great victory.

Old Cast Clouts and Old Rotten Rags
(The value of the valueless)

Jeremiah 38.11 "Tattered cast off clothes", or, as the Authorised Version has it, so much more vividly, "Old cast clouts and old rotten rags".

The hero of this story of Jeremiah's rescue from the dungeon was an Ethiopian slave — not a person of any consequence. He was, like all of his kind, despised, the butt of every would-be wit. No one would have expected Ebed-melech to bother very much when Jeremiah was lowered into the mud of a dungeon shaped like a bottle — dark, filthy, with no possible escape.

Nobody else bothered. It did not pay to bother about a prophet in disgrace at court. But Ebed-melech, with great courage, approached the King to plead for Jeremiah's life. Perhaps in sheer surprise at his effrontery, the King gave him his request, and with thirty men and strong cords, he went and drew the prophet out of the filthy prison. But first, thinking of how the ropes would pull and tear at the prisoner's arms, this despised black slave drew "old cast clouts and old rotten rags" from the store house to pad Jeremiah's armholes, where the cords would catch.

What a sensitive, sympathetic, thoughtful thing to do. To remember Jeremiah at all was much. To approach the King for him was more. But what lifts this story out of the ordinary are the old cast clouts and old rotten rags.

Let the text remind us of three things:

1. The usefulness of the apparently useless. We Scots are accused of being economical. We are, and I'm not ashamed of it. Waste is wicked. To use scraps of food, scraps of cloth, scraps of wood, scraps of anything, is a Godly occupation. Nothing is wasted in nature. Every drop of water is used over and over again. Every fallen leaf goes into the next year's growth. "Indestructibility of matter", call it what you will, is another name for the saving habit of God. It seems odd that when Jesus fed the five thousand, He should worry about the crumbs — but He did. He was stating one of God's own laws when he said, "Gather up the fragments which remain, that nothing be lost."

Conservation, the fight against pollution is thoroughly

Godly. The waste products, the scrap, the effluent, the paper which disfigure our countryside and poison our rivers should, in nearly every case, be retained and used. In how many cases progressive firms have found by-products to be more profitable than the original manufacture.

What is true physically is true spiritually. Once, a great preacher, Dr McIntosh McKay, was in my congregation in Glasgow. I wilted when I saw him, for I knew my sermon was weak and confused. Afterwards he came to see me and he thanked me. I said, "Now, Dr McKay, you know and I know that that was a miserable rag of a sermon." Honesty and kindness struggled in him for a little. Honesty finally triumphed, and then he brightened. "But God can use rags, you know." It is true. Like someone making a patchwork quilt, God can use little bits of service, tiny scraps of helpfulness. He can use you and me.

The old cast clouts and old rotten rags show the usefulness of the seemingly useless.

2. They also show us the bigness of little things.

What makes a day for us? It is not receiving £1000, an invitation to Buckingham Palace — although these things are not to be despised! It is the handclasp of a friend, the kiss of a child, the smile from a stranger.

All the time it was of little things the Christ spoke — a lost coin, a lost sheep, a fallen sparrow, a lily, a cup of cold water, a widow's mite. When at last He sought to tell of God's huge tenderness, it was a morsel of bread He took, and a sip of wine. Ever since, these little things have spoken of the greatest thing in the world — the love of God for man.

It wasn't much that Ebed-melech remembered to send down padding for the ropes, but Jeremiah noted the little extra touch and was thankful for it and set it down for all generations to learn by.

The usefulness of the useless; the bigness of little things; and —

3. The beauty of ugly things.

Those who have been at a removal or in the aftermath of a jumble sale know that there is nothing uglier than old rags or clothes past their first youth. But when Jeremiah saw the bundle of old cast clouts and old rotten rags — soft with age — coming down with the ropes, we can be sure he said the Jewish equivalent of "Lovely" and blessed the kind heart of Ebedmelech who had thought of them.

Christ was very quick to see beauty where nobody else could — a ridiculous little man up a tree, a faded, skittish frivol at the well, a leper, a lunatic. In each Jesus saw a beauty hidden from other eyes. And when He came to die, it was no lovely way He chose, but the most cruel and brutal kind of execution. We make crosses now of gold and silver and polished wood. But the first Cross was not like that. It was a rough thing, disgusting and horrible. But it became the means of our redemption and the proof of God's fathomless love.

As we live nearer to it and to Him who died upon it, we shall find the usefulness of the useless, the bigness of little things, the beauty of unlovely things. We shall find ourselves used as was this slave of long ago, who served God and his brother with old cast clouts and old rotten rags.

———— · ————

What Is There In It For Me?
(The reward for serving God)

Job 1.9 (RSV) "Does Job fear God for naught?"

"What is there in it for me?" "Can you make it worth my while?" "Any perks?" We are increasingly familiar with that kind of question in our nothing-for-nothing sort of world.

Can these questions be asked about religion? If people go to church and give to the Church and live a good life, do they get something in return? Does goodness pay? That is the sort of question with which the Book of Job is concerned. Job was the pride and joy of God's heart. God says to Satan, "Have you considered my servant Job? You will find no one like him on earth, a man of blameless and upright life, who fears God and sets his face against wrongdoing." Satan admits all that, but goes on to say in effect, "Well he may. He is doing very well out of it. He is being well paid for his efforts. Has not Job good reason to be God-fearing?" The jibe hurts God and He decides on a brave experiment. He gives Satan power to take away Job's wealth and health and sons and daughters; "And then," says God, "we'll see." The issue of it, of course, is that Job remains faithful. "Behold, he will slay me: I have no hope; yet I will defend my ways to his face." "Shall we receive good at the hand of God, and shall we not receive evil?" The whole book is taken up with proving that God does not reward goodness by health, prosperity and a long life. The conclusion of Job is that goodness does not pay.

Who can doubt that? Some kinds of badness do, indeed, cause the doers suffering, but we have all seen the wicked flourish like the green bay tree. We have all seen the righteous suffer sickness, pain, poverty and sorrow. If that be so, why should we bother with God at all? The pews in most churches are hard, the open air is inviting, we could use the money we give. Why waste time and money on an activity which yields no profit or reward?

One of the arguments for obeying and serving God is that, though we do not thereby guarantee for ourselves long life, health, wealth and happiness, we do make sure of heaven. A man who had been a monk for 13 years said that a monk's bed was hard to lie on, but sweet to die on; which was the reward of a monk's life. He goes into the monastery to learn how to die. If the old monk is right — if, in return for putting up with a hard bed and a vegetable diet, people can purchase an eternity of heaven which they might lose if they worked in a factory and got married, then they are foolish if they do not opt for the hard bed — and a single one at that. On this basis, once the reality of heaven and how it is to be achieved is accepted, it is just plain silly not to pay the price. Of course, if it can be got even cheaper — if heaven can be bought at a cut rate by getting one's name on the Communion Roll of a Parish Church and dropping in to Morning Service when it is suitable, one is on to a good thing. But, of course, this can't be done.

Please do not mistake me. I believe with all my heart that the most satisfactory life in the world is that lived in obedience to God, whether it is outwardly prosperous or not. I believe also with all my heart in heaven; that God in His love and mercy has prepared us things far better than we could ask or think. But God does not give prosperity here and joy yonder as a reward for our good behaviour. He rejects and repudiates any service or obedience or worship that is offered to Him in hope of rewards in this life or the life to come. If we go to church only if God makes it worth while for us with "perks" denied to others; if we go because there is something in it for us which we would miss if we did not put in our customary appearance; then we would be better at home.

The *motive* for the worship of God, for the service of Christ, and the only proper motive, is gratitude for what God has done for us. Until the Church can shake out those who belong to it for what they can get out of it — or think they can get out of it — in this world or the world to come, the Church will be hampered and hamstrung in her witness. For those who are in it for what they hope to get out of it will put in as little as they can get away with. It is only when we know what God has done for us, and in gratitude worship and serve Him, that nothing will be too much to give or to do for His sake Who has done all things well for us. And there will be the sort of joy and spontaneity and lavishness in our worship and in our service which will reflect the joyous and lavish spontaneity of Christ.

"Does Job fear God for naught?" Do you? If not, you do not serve Him as you ought.

---·---

Is There Any Word From The Lord?
(The need for God's truth)

Jeremiah 37.17 "Is there any word from the Lord?"

King Hezekiah had plenty of advisers — wise men, prophets, members of the Cabinet — and all of them gave him the same advice: what they thought he wanted most to hear. For a time he was satisfied with their flattery. Then suddenly he was sick of them and their servile ways. He knew they had been making a fool of him. Now he wanted the truth, however unpleasant it might be. But whom could he trust to tell him the truth? There was only one man — the prophet Jeremiah whom he had got rid of. He had thrown him into a bottle dungeon because he dared to predict doom. The King knew that Jeremiah feared no man, so he sent for him. Jeremiah was brought out of prison, up the back stairs of the Palace, into the presence of the King. What a picture! On the one side, the King in all his magnificence, but worried and afraid. Facing him, the prophet in his wretched rags, with the prison pallor on his face and the smell of the dungeon clinging to him.

But the first one to speak and to make a request was not the prisoner but the King. As soon as they were alone, he blurted it out. "Is there any word from the Lord?" This was what the King wanted; no longer the half-truths and easy speeches that comfort cruel men, but the truth of God as this man of God heard it — even though it stung and seared.

"Is there any word from the Lord?" — any authentic news from beyond the relativities of this world? Is not this what we all long for? We get plenty of words, in all conscience —

magazines and newspapers, radio and television. Our eyes, minds and hearts are assailed by a veritable torrent of words from the time we open our eyes in the morning till we fall asleep; but somehow none seems to answer our deepest questions or meet our deepest needs. All seem to be little more than the speculations and rumours of men, as they stand, wistfully longing for some true news from One who is really able to help our world and able to help us. "Is there any word from the Lord?"

This, of course is what brings us Sunday by Sunday to church — not the music, not the friends we meet, but the hunger for something to be found nowhere else; for some word from the other side. This is the unspoken question we each of us brings to every church service. "Is there any word from the Lord?" This is what gives the Bible its awesome authority, its unique place; that time and time again, God has taken these words and spoken them as His own to seeking human hearts. Our churches would have crumbled long ago, but for the fact that, amidst the welter of words — mere human words — we sometimes hear an authentic word from the Lord. I would not be a preacher of the Gospel for five minutes if I did not believe with all my heart that sometimes, through a preacher's voice and words, the listening ear can hear the word for him or her from God Himself.

What is the word we seek which only God can give? First, forgiveness. Even if we do not mention sin any more, there is that which lies on the conscience of us all. There are the wrongs we cannot right. Nobody can help, save Him who can say, "Neither do I condemn you. Go and do not sin again."

Then there are the burdens of loneliness, childlessness, too much work or too little — the burdens which no one can help to ease, but only a voice which says, "My grace is sufficient for you." That helps when we remember that the Speaker himself knew loneliness and pain and disappointment and a Cross.

Or sorrow? When life tumbles in, and he or she is dead, then we may be grateful to those who try to comfort us, but they cannot help. The only word which can help then is, "I am the Resurrection and the Life; he who believes in me, though he die, yet shall he live."

And when the last darkness draws near for us, man's word cannot help, for it cannot reach. Nothing can help then unless the words of Him who came from God and has gone to God, "Let not your hearts be troubled." "Be of good cheer. I have overcome the world."

It is a wonderful Gospel, for it is the only Gospel — the only good news in our fearful world, in our stumbling, perplexing lives. It is the Gospel of God's word for our salvation and the salvation of the world.

Jeremiah did his best to answer King Hezekiah's timid question, "Is there any word from the Lord?" but not for a thousand years was the true answer given, not until the Word was made flesh and dwelt among us. He is what God has to say to the world. He is the answer to everyone's deepest question, "Is there any word from the Lord?"

Absalom
(The yearning to be remembered)

2 Samuel 18.18 (RSV) "Absalom set up for himself a pillar, for he said, 'I have no son to keep my name in remembrance'."

There is no other book which knows the human heart like the Bible. As we read it — if we read it — over and over again we recognise ourselves, our own hopes and fears and dreams and longings, see ourselves, as it were, in a mirror.

All of us know exactly how Absalom felt. He craved to be remembered. We all do. We have never come to terms with our mortality. We all rebel against the shortness of our lives. We find it intolerable that such complex and marvellously fashioned creatures as we are should be extinguished after 70 years or less, when an artery less than a quarter of an inch across blocks. We do our best to prolong our lives so far as we can, but knowing that we shall finally fail, we use whatever means are open to us to leave behind us some memorials, something to tell those who come after us that we have lived.

Obviously we live on in some measure in the hearts and minds of the younger people who will survive us. Most of us remember our parents, our aunts and uncles. Some remember at least one grandparent and a few their great grandparents. But before that we hardly even know their names.

So knowing that, we try to devise other means whereby we shall be remembered. We erect tombs or raise memorials or set up charitable trusts. For a time they do guarantee a kind of remembrance, but only for a time. The Taj Mahal, the pyramids, the sphinx, the great monuments of the Incas in South America have withstood the ravages of time, but few now know whose memory they were meant to perpetuate:

"I met a traveller from an antique land
Who said, 'Two vast and trunkless legs of stone
Stand in the desert.'
And on a pedestal these words appear,
'My name is Osymandius, King of Kings.
Look on my works, ye mighty, and despair.'
Nothing beside remains. Round the decay
Of that colossal wreck, boundless and bare
The lone and level sands stretch far away."

Like Osymandius, Absalom raised his pillar in the hope that by it he would be remembered, but his hope was vain. When 2nd Samuel was written, the pillar had crumbled and decayed, but the site was still called Absalom's Place. But now all trace is gone and no one remembers where this pillar was by which Absalom meant for ever to be remembered.

And yet, of course, Absalom is remembered, even in these days when few people know their Bible. It is not many years since a novel *Absalom, my Son* came out. Why and how is Absalom remembered after 3000 years? By his pillar? It is gone and its creation forgotten. I doubt if many of you had heard of it until today! By his wars? No, for they all ended in defeat and disgrace. For his good looks? They had disappeared in a few days after his burial. By his descendants? No, for he had no sons. But he *is* remembered. How?

I'll tell you. Because of the heartbroken cry of the old father he despised and sought to overthrow. He is remembered for this reason — that David loved him with an understanding and all-forgiving tenderness which made him mourn the victory that took the lad's life. David cared nothing for the crushing of the rebellion. The only question he asked of the despatch riders was, "Is the young man Absalom safe?" and when he knew the bitter truth there came from him the agonised cry that has echoed down the ages, finding a response in many a sorrowing heart. "O my son Absalom, my son, my son Absalom. Would I had died instead of you, O Absalom, my son, my son!"

That cry will move hearts as long as the world shall last, and by it, and by it alone, will Absalom be remembered.

The meaning for us is plain. Our value lies not in what we make, nor in what we achieve, but in the affection and regard in which we are held by some few who love us, despite our faults and follies. Most of all, our value, our hope of being remembered, lies in the love of God for us all.

The modern problem is the problem of man. What is man? Is he an accident in a soul-less universe, or is he a son of the Most High God? Behind all the debates in Parliament, behind all the international problems, all the problems of medical ethics — euthanasia, abortion and the like — lies this. What is man?

And the Bible gives the answer. Man is a being of infinite value, of eternal worth, not because of his cleverness nor his power nor his goodness, but because the Lord God loved him, loved him enough to send His Son to die for him — and loves him still. "God so loved the world that he gave his only begotten Son, that whoever believes in him *should not perish* but have eternal life."

David would have died for Absalom, for was he not his son.

Christ died for us all.

We shall no longer be haunted by Absalom's pitiful yearning to be remembered if we know that our names are written in the Lamb's Book of Life, not of our deserving, nor by our merit, but by the infinite mercy of God. Our guarantee of eternity is grounded not on the failing memory of men, not in stones that crumble, nor in memorials which disappear, but on the everlasting and astounding love of God for us all in Jesus Christ.

> "Nor death, nor life, nor earth nor hell,
> Nor time's destroying sway,
> Can e'er efface us from *his* heart
> Or make *his* love decay."

Absalom said "I have no son to keep my name in remembrance."

Jesus said, "I go to prepare a place for you, that where I am you may be also."

Jacob and Joseph
(Our hopes for our children)

Genesis 49.22-25 (RSV) "Joseph is a fruitful bough — the archers fiercely attacked him, shot at him, and harassed him sorely; yet his bow remained unmoved, his arms were made agile by the hands of the Mighty One, by the God of your father who will help you, by God Almighty who will bless you."

These words were spoken by Jacob, Joseph's father. When he was young, Jacob acted on the principle that the Lord helps those who help themselves. He had helped himself by fair means and foul. Do you remember the mean way in which he had used Esau's hunger to buy from him his birthright with a mess of pottage, his inheritance for a bowl of lentil soup? Egged on by his fond mother, he had used a stratagem to steal his father's blessing. Even his religion had been self-centred. At Bethel, after his dream of the ladder set up to heaven, he had proposed his famous bargain to God — if you will take care of me and bring me safe home again, then I will make you my God. When he saw Rachel, he wanted her for his wife and made sure that he got her in the end. Living with his father-in-law, he had abused his hospitality to enrich himself by every trick and stratagem. Jacob knew what he wanted out of life and made sure that he got it.

Now he was old and done and he knew that he must soon die, and he wanted nothing. Perhaps it was the death of Rachel which had taken the heart out of him, had broken him of his greed and ambition, had made him see the unimportance of the things he had coveted and schemed for. When she had died, something vital had died in him too.

Now all his hopes and ambition were centred on his sons. He looked round on them — Judah, the greatest of them all; Benjamin, in giving birth to whom Rachel had died; but most of all his eyes kept returning to Joseph, his favourite.

Joseph had been idolised and pampered as a boy, mourned through the long, lost years, and finally found again, the Grand Vizier of Egypt and the instrument of his family's deliverance from famine. Joseph had come a long way from the raw, boastful lad who had excited his brothers' envy. He had done well. He had wealth, power, position, influence, had developed a largeness of spirit which had enabled him to forgive his brothers. He was a great man. The others wondered what more his father could wish for him — he had everything already.

Then his father spoke. "Joseph is a fruitful bough." How true, they said. Then Jacob shows that he has learned his lesson, for he foretells that Joseph will have no easy time of it — the man of integrity never has. "The archers fiercely attacked him, shot at him, and harassed him sorely." Jacob does not expect and does not ask, that his dead son shall have an easy time nor freedom from attack or opposition. Let him have his share of reverses and his dangers. Only, he prays, let him have two things which will enable him to face them — courage for the evil day and the assurance of the nearness and the love of God.

So — what about us? What would we choose for ourselves if some fairy godmother appeared to grant us three wishes?

Health? Is there anything more important?

Money? How much easier life would be if we only had enough!

Popularity? It is nice to be respected, to be well thought of, to have some place and influence in the community.

Yet, as we grow older, we begin to see through popularity and power and we grow less ambitious for riches. We learn that this world's empty glory can cost us too dear. We can learn even to take our share of pain and sickness. If we have any maturity at all, we grow less greedy, are content with much less than once we wanted.

But even when every fond ambition has perished so far as we ourselves are concerned, we're apt to say we want the best for our children and if we ask ourselves what we mean by "the best", we find that we think of it in the same old terms — health, money, a position of influence, a happy and comfortable home. Even although, as we look back, we see quite clearly that conflict, opposition, sorrow, even danger, all had their place in our own lives, that curiously we are the better for them, that without them our lives would have been tasteless, flat and enervating, even though we know all that, we persist in wanting to shield our children from them. We hope that somehow they will get off lightly and have the sort of soft and easy life which in our heart of hearts we know would have distorted us.

Perhaps we have something to learn from Jacob. To ask for ourselves and for those who come after, not a good time, not success or happiness, but only courage to face what must be faced, and integrity not to yield to temptation, and steadfastness not to whine or whimper when trouble does come.

It is easy to say all this, all too easy, but not so easy to do. Jacob knew it, and so, for his well beloved son he asked for one thing more — that he might know the touch of God upon his life and find in Him a strength not his own. Arms "made agile by the hands of the Mighty One, by the God of your father who will help you, by God Almighty who will bless you."

Are you still doubtful? "Art thou afraid His power will cease when comes thy evil day?" Look then at Christ and at His Cross, for He has taken a road harder than any we can be asked to tread, and when that road ended in darkness and pain, He was still sure that the hands of God were near. "Father, into your hands," He cried. Taught by Him we may learn to say and believe:

> "My times are in thy hand:
> Why should I doubt or fear?
> My Father's hand will never cause
> His child a needless tear."

Neither it will.

"Joseph is a fruitful bough. The archers fiercely attacked him, shot at him, and harassed him sorely; yet his bow remained unmoved, his arms were made agile, by the hands of the Mighty One, by the God of your father who will help you, by God Almighty who will bless you."

Courage, the touch of the hands of God, His help and His blessing. Let us ask those for ourselves and for those dear to us and ask no more.